DEVIL'S ADVOCATES

T0341705

DEVIL'S ADVOCATES is a series of books devoted to exploring the classics of horror cinema. Contributors to the series come from the fields of teaching, academia, journalism and fiction, but all have one thing in common: a passion for the horror film and a desire to share it with the widest possible audience.

'The admirable Devil's Advocates series is not only essential – and fun – reading for the serious horror fan but should be set texts on any genre course.'
Dr Ian Hunter, Reader in Film Studies, De Montfort University, Leicester

'Auteur Publishing's new Devil's Advocates critiques on individual titles... offer bracingly fresh perspectives from passionate writers. The series will perfectly complement the BFI archive volumes.' **Christopher Fowler, *Independent on Sunday***

'Devil's Advocates has proven itself more than capable of producing impassioned, intelligent analyses of genre cinema... quickly becoming the go-to guys for intelligent, easily digestible film criticism.' ***Horror Talk.com***

'Auteur Publishing continue the good work of giving serious critical attention to significant horror films.' ***Black Static***

 DevilsAdvocatesbooks

 DevilsAdBooks

DEVIL'S ADVOCATES

THE SILENCE OF THE LAMBS

BARRY FORSHAW

Acknowledgments

For their invaluable help: Judith Forshaw, Ali Karim.

First published in 2013, reprinted 2014 by
Auteur, 24 Hartwell Crescent, Leighton Buzzard LU7 1NP
www.auteur.co.uk
Copyright © Auteur 2013

Series design: Nikki Hamlett at Cassels Design
Set by Cassels Design www.casselsdesign.co.uk
Printed and bound by CPI Group (UK) Ltd, Croydon, CR0 4YY

British Library Cataloguing-in-Publication Data
A catalogue record for this book is available from the British Library

ISBN 978-1-906733-65-0
ISBN 978-1-906733-98-8 (e-book)

CONTENTS

INTRODUCTION

History can repeat itself. Just as Thomas Harris's novels *Red Dragon* (published 1981) and *The Silence of the Lambs* (1988) represented a double whammy that permanently reconfigured the crime fiction genre (and, as a by-product, the entire field of horror fiction), so the subsequent successful films of the books performed a concomitant shift in popular crime/horror cinema. *The Silence of the Lambs* (1991), in particular, inaugurated a sea change in thriller cinema – a change the effects of which are being felt to this day (not least in freighting in extra layers of texture and resonance into narrative structure).

Many writers – whether in the crime or horror field – envy Thomas Harris his unparalleled storytelling abilities. Harris has long since gone beyond being merely a top-flight writer: he is now a brand, and his sanguinary serial killer novels are the defining works of the genre. His name is routinely (and, mostly, vainly) invoked for every new writer who attempts to cover the same territory. But there is only one Thomas Harris, and each novel (along with the inevitable film adaptations) featuring the super-intelligent aesthete and monster Hannibal Lecter is an event, nothing less. *Red Dragon* was the first book to introduce the cultivated serial killer, and its plot (including a unique symbiotic relationship between detective and prey) was very swiftly being imitated. *The Silence of the Lambs* took the phenomenon onto a whole new level. Clarice Starling is a trainee FBI agent, working hard to discipline mind and body. She is sent by her boss, Section Chief Jack Crawford, to interview the serial killer Hannibal Lecter, kept in the very tightest security, to see if he's prepared to help in the case of a killer using a similar modus operandi. But the inexperienced Clarice is no match for the Machiavellian Lecter, and he begins to play highly sophisticated mind games with her, while the other monster – the unincarcerated one – continues to ply his bloody trade.

It's not hard to see why this remarkable book achieved such acclaim: it is, quite simply, a tour de force. And while Lecter may not be like any serial killer who ever walked the earth (most are dull, stupid men from a less privileged social class than Lecter – and who could hardly lecture on Italian Renaissance art à la Lecter), he remains the most iconic super-criminal in modern fiction. Given the phenomenal success of Harris's novel, the author could certainly have survived a maladroit cinema adaptation when the inevitable movie was made. In fact, the author was lucky: director Jonathan Demme got everything right, orchestrating the tension with the skill of a latter-day Alfred Hitchcock, and introducing elements hitherto under-utilised in the crime/horror field – elements to be examined and celebrated in this study. The real success of the movie, however, lies in the casting of Jodie Foster, impeccably incarnating the out-of-her-depth Clarice, and Anthony Hopkins, masterly as the urbane Lecter (even undercutting the Hollywood cliché of casting all well-spoken intelligent villains as British by utilising an impeccable American accent). Above all the film (like the novel) is intelligent, a sharp contrast to most contemporary Hollywood fare.

But the first outing for Thomas Harris's music- and art-loving psychopath, *Red Dragon*, is as comprehensively gripping as its successor. As well as the brilliantly delineated villain, there is a strong hero in Special Agent Will Graham, assigned to such cases as Lecter's because of his ability to intuitively place himself in the mind of monsters. As Harris had demonstrated in previous thrillers (such as *Black Friday* [1975], with its ever-more-relevant terrorist atrocity theme), his grasp of narrative structure is unswerving, and the careful, precision-timed parcelling out of plot information is one of the author's trademarks. But while others have attempted to imitate such tropes, none possess Harris's consummate mastery of characterisation – everybody in the novel is limned with painterly skill, whether in a few well-chosen lines or (like the monstrous Lecter) at satisfying length. Readers quickly realised they might forget the million and one imitators that swiftly followed: Thomas Harris was the *locus classicus*.

Red Dragon may have finally been filmed by Brett Ratner under its actual title with Anthony Hopkins, now a shade too old for the role, but the first screen incarnation of American serial killer Hannibal Lecter was another British (and also Celtic) actor, Brian Cox, in Michael Mann's chillingly effective reading of the novel, re-named *Manhunter* (1986). There are those who prefer Cox's more neutral, understated reading of the role, but such views often go hand-in-hand with a claim that whoever is extolling Cox's performance knew about the virtues of Mann's initially underrated movie before it became the *succès d'estime* it now is.

This study will attempt to contextualise the work of Thomas Harris, demonstrating how the films made of his books (most notably Demme's *The Silence of the Lambs*) are as crucial to his success and critical standing as the original novels, and how Harris channelled existing horror tropes to create a new, durable hybrid of the crime and horror genres.

HANNIBAL'S PRECURSORS

Over the years, popular literature has produced more than its share of murderers who qualify for the description of serial killers, but the phenomenon is a more recent one in the cinema. In 1959, the writer Robert Bloch was inspired by the gruesome case of the Wisconsin mass murderer Ed Gein, with his keepsakes of bones and human skin (Gein was a killer who Thomas Harris was later to study in his time at the FBI's Behavioural Science Unit). Bloch, a highly proficient novelist who had made his mark writing for the influential horror pulp magazine *Weird Tales*, transmuted elements of the Gein case into the phenomenally successful *Psycho* (published 1959), reconfiguring the real-life Gein as the chubby, unprepossessing mother's boy Norman Bates, who dispatches a variety of victims in gruesome fashion (beheading one with a knife – a death famously changed in the subsequent film). Bloch had in fact worked on the television show fronted by the director Alfred Hitchcock, but was unaware that the successful anonymous bidder for the rights to his novel was indeed the great English film-maker — and it was Hitchcock's adaptation (1960) which was to lay down the parameters for a variety of genres: the serial killer movie, the slasher film (substituting for Hitchcock's complex and nuanced characters a series of interchangeable victims to be bloodily dispatched) and the modern big-budget horror film which utilises above-the-title stars rather than the journeyman actors who had populated such fare previously. But above all else, Hitchcock and his talented screenwriter Joseph Stefano created a template for the intelligent, richly developed and charismatic fictional serial killer in their version of Norman Bates (developed and characterised to a far greater degree than the protagonist of Robert Bloch's source novel). Hitchcock's film – his greatest commercial success – was to influence a generation of film-makers and writers; among them Thomas Harris.

PRESENTABLE SERIAL KILLERS

The Norman Bates of Hitchcock's film was no longer obese, but a slim, nervous and attractive young man. For exigent reasons of plotting (Bates' identity as the film's serial killer – now known to the world – was cannily concealed from original audiences unfamiliar with the novel), his madness and psychotic ruthlessness share many of the

Psycho's *Norman Bates (Anthony Perkins), without whom...*

elements that Harris was later to develop in Hannibal Lecter. Both Anthony Perkins in *Psycho* and Anthony Hopkins in *The Silence of the Lambs* are personable and good-looking, and display a ready charm – although Hopkins' killer, of course, is never seen by audience or characters without the knowledge of his murderous nature, so the apparent charm is deeply sinister.

Both men are cultivated – Lecter with his knowledge of art, cuisine and the humanities in general, Bates with more discreet cultural references; in Vera Miles' fraught traversal of the Bates household, she finds in Norman's room a record of a Beethoven symphony as well as a child's cot – emblematic of the non-homogenous, warring elements of Norman's mind. And the actor Perkins subtly conveys the sense that he is more intelligent than any of the other characters in the film. There is also, of course, the feminine qualities that both actors bring to their serial killers – more pronounced in the case of Perkins, but Hopkins' forensic understanding and putative sympathy for Jodie Foster's Clarice shows what might be read as a 'feminine' intuitiveness towards the nuances of a vulnerable woman's personality.

Leaving aside these character components, Hitchcock also inaugurated two key elements which were to be utilised in many subsequent serial killer movies (not least

Jonathan Demme's film): the foregrounding of a dark and terrifying journey into the mind of a psychopath, treated with more medically plausible verisimilitude than had previously been seen in the cinema; and, secondly, the complex plotting, demanding sharp attention from the audience with revelations afforded at key intervals.

But if *Psycho* was an ancestor of Thomas Harris's series of serial killer novels and their subsequent films, there were other memorable manifestations of the phenomenon along the way, such as Jack Smight's *No Way to Treat a Lady* (1968), in which Rod Steiger is allowed to build up a considerable head of steam (something the actor, characteristically, needed little persuasion to do) as a multiple murderer who assumes a variety of disguises while performing sexually motivated murders. Some of the disguises are bizarrely camp, such as an outrageous, distinctly non-PC gay character (who is, in fact, thwarted – one of the murderer's few failures in the film).

Where *No Way to Treat a Lady* might be said to prefigure the far more serious Hopkins portrayal of Lecter is the pronounced strain of black humour that is cannily employed throughout the film – murderous though the Steiger character may be, he is always (like Lecter) grimly entertaining, eloquent and often waspishly funny. The over-the-top denouement, however, in which Steiger largely squanders the impressive work he has done throughout the film, is not the kind of misstep to be found in any of the Hopkins Lecter portrayals – although a notable (and familiar) syndrome may be seen to be at work in the Welsh actor's subsequent versions of the character after the Demme film; the almost inevitable tendency to play things a little more broadly, and to point up the dark comedy of the material in a more ostentatious, less subtle fashion.

The serial killer film – before it was identified as a discrete and fecund sub-genre – produced some highly effective and memorable entries (along with many workaday efforts). Richard Fleischer's *The Boston Strangler* (1968) was a key example; the film (while utilising the fashionable split screen techniques of the day) cleverly adopted a low-key documentary approach, with a chillingly understated performance by Tony Curtis in the title role, the real-life killer Albert de Salvo. The acclaim for the film was echoed by that accorded to the same director's subsequent British-set *10 Rillington Place* (1971, the American Fleischer making a mini-speciality of the genre), which featured a highly intelligent, manipulative killer, John Christie (memorably played by

Richard Attenborough). The latter film's murders were firmly located within a British background, as were those in the last truly accomplished film by a British expatriate making a valedictory return, Alfred Hitchcock. The director had returned to his native shores (and Covent Garden just before its imminent conversion from market to tourist trap) to create in *Frenzy* (1972) another memorable serial killer, Robert Rusk (as played by Barry Foster with a predilection for using neckties in his sexually-motivated murders). To some extent, *Frenzy* is an enthusiastic continuation of the director's attempt to utilise the shock tactics of the horror film (as in *Psycho*), combining the pitch-black humour of much of the genre (also, of course, the director's own *métier*) with more grotesque, shocking elements than he had been previously disposed to explore – such as the hideous detail of a strangulation victim's protruding tongue (and a view of her exposed breasts beneath a torn-open blouse).

There were, of course, other serial killers in the cinema before Lecter (as discussed elsewhere), but the Hitchcock/Bloch-derived blueprint remains the lodestone. And although *Psycho* was to be considered a 'horror' rather than a 'crime' film, the director and the writer had worked repeatedly within the latter genre before. After *Psycho*, Hitchcock was to make the similarly horrific *The Birds* (1963), and Bloch was to remain ineluctably a horror writer thereafter, revisiting the well of *Psycho* with ever-diminishing returns in a series of variations on his most famous novel.

THE ASCENT OF HANNIBAL LECTER

We might describe Thomas Harris (born in 1940) as the JD Salinger of the thriller field, without the latter's attenuated drying-up of productivity, but with a degree of the late Salinger's reclusiveness. Harris, as is now well known, steadfastly refuses to give interviews; similarly, he declines to allow his publisher to organise signings for his new books, shunning all such promotional activities. The slim biographical details that are available concerning him afford readers a few paltry observations: Harris was an editor and reporter for Associated Press, and covered a variety of crime-related events both in North America and south of the border. The direction in which his fiction was decisively to take him – dark, psychological territory with a strong leavening of the horrific – was foreshadowed by the gruesome stories he is said to have sent as an aspiring writer to magazines such as *Argosy* while still attending university. However, his first novel, *Black Sunday*, suggested that his career would take a different turn, with more mainstream thriller subject matter concerned with a terrorist attack.

This extremely accomplished debut novel parleyed elements from the real-life murderous assaults by terrorists at the Munich Olympics, and the inevitable film of the book (1977) did some justice to Harris's novel. But it might be said that the book was a false dawn, at least in terms of the author's future direction – Harris's real metier (readers were to learn) was the serial killer novel, a genre that Harris may not have created, but which he brought to its finest fruition. Engaged in research for the book which became *Red Dragon* in 1981, Harris spent time researching at the Federal Bureau of Investigation's Behavioral Science Unit, where he paid particular attention to three notorious murderers, Ed Gein, Edmund Kemper and Richard Chase. Harris supplemented his study of the case files of these dangerous individuals with a trek to Italy for the trial of the killer (or killers) known as the 'Monster of Florence'. (The identity of 'Il Mostro di Firenze' was never satisfactorily settled – the guilt of those arraigned for the crime was much challenged at the time. Elements of this experience were transmuted into Harris's subsequent novel *Hannibal* in 1999.)

The effect of *Red Dragon* on crime and horror fiction was seismic, both artistically and commercially. Harris sets out his stall decisively and makes it quickly apparent that

Lecter is unlike most other fictional monsters we have encountered: he is well-read, charismatic and immensely polite. In fact, politeness is one of the key components of his baleful personality: those he considers 'impolite' (and his very personal interpretations of this transgression are wide-ranging) he kills – and, in fact, compounds the crime by eating them, accompanied by a suitable beverage. His prey are frequently other killers (prefiguring a literary slew of Lecter imitators), monsters who – unlike himself (as he sees it) – are mere murderers, without his 'redeeming' features such as a high IQ, impressive culinary skills (useful in preparations for his own delectation of the flesh of his victims) and an expert knowledge of Italian Renaissance art. In fact, one of Harris's signal achievements is the establishment of the character's unacknowledged *mauvais foi* – the monumental, smug self-deception he practices to maintain a lofty distance between himself and those he considers to be ordinary killers: or worse, ordinary killers who lack manners.

MORIARTY'S HEIR

Needless to say, Hannibal Lecter's massive intelligence, and the military precision of his planning (the latter owing something to both Arthur Conan Doyle's Sherlock Holmes and the latter's nemesis, the equally intelligent Professor James Moriarty) means that on any sliding scale of atrocity, Lecter is far, far worse than his lower-IQ rivals. But the essence of the character's lack of self-knowledge is, perhaps, of a piece with his own essential unknowability; despite the frequent articulations he grants of his own cold-blooded ethos, the only thing that those who deal with him (and, *inter alia*, the reader) really know about Lecter is the almost cosmic depth of his amorality (his is an unforgiving universe which has its own parameters of right and wrong, but one that is markedly different from normal people – like, presumably, ourselves).

Of course, as with Holmes and Moriarty, any villain is only as good as the detective set against him (or vice versa), and in Will Graham (and, later, Starling), Harris pulls off the enviable trick of creating a 'good', moral character who maintains the attention of the reader as rigorously as the larger-than-life villain. We become almost as fascinated by the vulnerable Will Graham as we do with Lecter, and feel anxiety when the latter (for the first time) begins to play the destabilising mind games that are his principal stock in trade — Lecter enjoys few things more than anatomising the personalities of the representatives of the law he deals with and then attempting to strip them down in ruthlessly forensic fashion. We are quite as concerned with the survival and mental health of Will Graham as we are in his pursuit of the 'lesser' serial killer Francis Dollarhyde (for the capture of whom Graham attempts to enlist Lecter's aid). The latter, in fact, is characterised with precisely the same chilling élan that Harris utilises for the other characters, and chapters devoted to Dollarhyde's backstory are among the most compelling in *Red Dragon*.

There is a canny synthesis of different elements in this quite remarkable novel: on the surface, a nonpareil orchestration of narrative tension (with a panache which has rarely been seen before in popular literature), married to a strip-mining of character that has the richness of nuance of more respectable literary fiction. But perhaps the most intriguing element of the novel is the utilisation (and examination) of notions of reportage, in which the author calls upon his journalistic background to lay before the reader a veritable army of facts, paraded somewhat in the fashion of the pioneering technique of British writer Frederick Forsyth in *The Day of the Jackal* (published 1971) – but with far greater attention to psychological detail. Without any apparent tendentiousness, Lecter's (and Harris's) minatory universe is fashioned from these initially disparate elements and fused into a fictional construct that makes most other similar entries in the field seem thin gruel. Such was the accomplishment of the novel (not to mention its prodigious commercial success) that a film adaptation was inevitable. But could it do justice to the novel?

MANHUNTER: HANNIBAL'S SCREEN DEBUT

With the film *Manhunter*, the director Michael Mann and the actor Brian Cox decisively marked out the territory for future appearances by Hannibal Lecter. Not least for the truthfulness of its performances, it is impossible to imagine a more strongly cast version of Thomas Harris' 1981 novel *Red Dragon* than Mann's remarkable film, boasting such actors as William Peterson as reluctant (and damaged) FBI agent Will Graham,

Tom Noonan, delivering a truly unsettling reading of serial killer Francis Dollarhyde and the affecting Joan Allen as the latter's luckless blind associate. Actors (and writer/ director) apart, there is one particular craftsman involved in the making of the film whose contribution is in some ways as critical as that of anyone else involved with it: the accomplished cinematographer Dante Spinotti. It was a particularly happy combination of circumstances that led to the hiring of this doyen of Italian directors of photography, not least the fact that an Italian production company, that of the formidable Dino di Laurentiis, owned the rights to the novel (the name change was dictated by di Laurentiis because of the proximity in release to the misfiring Michael Cimino/Mickey Rourke film *Year of the Dragon* [1985]). Spinotti's contribution is crucial, and is evident in every frame. *Manhunter* is a film of surfaces (in both a physical and metaphorical sense), with the marriage of light, shade and texture with the carefully calculated production design (forensically created by Michael Mann and Mel Bourne, with a Vincente Minnelli-like attention to the psychological properties of colour) resulting in the film's chilly, unique look.

BLOODY COLOUR PALETTES

It is not without significance that the high-gloss surfaces and the almost expressionistic use of colour are such a key element in the film. Italy, birthplace of the cinematographer Spinotti, of course, is the home of the blood-soaked *giallo* – a Latin sub-genre of gruesome thriller that must be considered in any discussion of films based on the work of Thomas Harris.

While other popular genres utilised by Italian directors are Latin variations on established formulae (the American Western, the Hammer horror film) it might be argued that the *giallo* is unusual: a home-grown product synthesising a variety of elements from other countries in classic exploitation fashion, but fashioning something particularly individual which in itself proved immensely influential (a parallel might be drawn here with serious music: Igor Stravinsky influencing Bela Bartok, who in turn influenced Stravinsky). And *Manhunter* can in fact be read as a classic *giallo*, often looking like nothing so much as the legitimate offspring of the two great *gialli* directors,

Mario Bava and Dario Argento. Both these film-makers favoured the use of coloured filters (and even saturated film stock as in Argento's influential *Suspiria* [1977]) along with loving, caressing panning shots across strikingly designed modern architecture -- elements to be found in abundance in *Manhunter*. Crucial component of the *gialli* to be borrowed for that film, *Silence of the Lambs* and other Harris adaptations are discussed in a succeeding section, not least the fact that the genre's serial killers – as with Hannibal Lecter – commit their multiple murders for reasons other than psychosexual compulsion (despite the deceptive eroticism of the genre with its nude or barely-dressed female victims bloodily dispatched).

INFLUENCE OF THE GIALLO

The Italian horror film was probably the finest flower of that country's popular cinema, but of equal long-term significance is the genre of the stylish murder thriller, the *giallo*. The most adroit exponents of the latter fields (apart from the groundbreaking Riccardo Freda) were the veteran Mario Bava, the younger Dario Argento, Sergio Martino and the less talented Lucio Fulci. Once a despised genre (principally because of the crass dubbing to which the films were invariably subjected outside of Italy), *gialli* have undergone a major critical re-assessment, with their visual stylishness and bizarre plotting now celebrated. These grisly whodunits, inspired by the yellow (*giallo*)-jacketed thriller 1930s/40s paperbacks that enjoyed immense success among Italian readers, represented something of a sleight-of-hand in their strategies. With their high-gloss surfaces (widescreen and lurid colour are almost always *de rigueur* for the genre), the essential paradigms were a sumptuously photographed series of murder set-pieces in upscale apartments (with the victims usually beautifully dressed, sensuous women), apparently committed by a sex-obsessed psychopath. The murder weapon is customarily a knife, brandished in a black-gloved hand. But this twisted psychopathology motive is almost invariably a red herring: mammon is usually at the centre of the killings, with greed and financial gain being the leitmotif as the source of the bloodletting (the *reductio ad absurdum* of this schematic is Mario Bava's *Ecologia del Delitto/A Bay of Blood* [1971]), where the treatment of the murder motivation is almost absurdly casual). In the same fashion that Thomas Harris co-opted horror fiction tropes for the crime novel (thereby altering reader perception of both genres), it is evident that the films made of the writer's work (in particular, *The Silence of the Lambs*) similarly utilise and reconfigure elements of the *giallo*, notably the sumptuously-appointed surfaces, synthesis of multiple genres and gruesome murder set pieces.

So what sort of work populated the genre? The film that might be considered one of the first *gialli*, Mario Bava's *Sei Donne per l'Assassino/Blood and Black Lace* (1964), is comfortably the director's most influential film on the cinema of other countries – and a key work in the field, with narrative and visual tropes that instantly became templates for the glossy catalogues of mayhem in the films of Argento, Sergio Martino, Umberto Lenzi and others.

Thomas Harris's initially fragile but intelligent Clarice Starling, however, would not be a natural fit as the protagonist for a *giallo*. In the *giallo* field, fetishistic imagery is the order of the day, and those looking for a more enlightened, feminist view of female sexuality should look elsewhere (in fact, it would probably be a good idea for such individuals to ignore the *giallo* genre altogether). Another signal difference between the genre and the films of Thomas Harris's books lies in the area of plotting.

For all their delirious visual invention, plotting is not the strong suit of the *giallo* – what mostly serves for plotting is a tortuous stitching together of disparate narrative elements to provide integument for the blood-drenched set pieces. Yet the same charge might be levelled at the masterpieces of Hitchcock; except that the English director was canny enough to hire the best screenwriters to provide such texture along with psychological verisimilitude – another element only fitfully present in most *gialli*. However, such films as *The Silence of the Lambs* incorporate quality writing and rigorous plotting along with exuberant staging, sanguinary inventiveness and constant visual flourishes.

MURDER AND *MISE EN SCÈNE*

In supplements created for the DVD release of *Manhunter*, Dante Spinotti speaks enthusiastically of his director's fondness for the visual, married to a rigorous organisation of every element of *mise-en-scène* in the film. It is undoubtedly true that

Manhunter's cult status owes as much to this visual intelligence as it does to the carefully chosen rock soundtrack, a key element of Michael Mann's creative approach since the days of the superficial but undeniably seductive television series *Miami Vice* (1984–1990), with the same attention to surface and patina that would characterise *Manhunter*. But if Mann and his cinematographer had been obliged to photograph performances of a low voltage, the film would not enjoy the cult status that it now does. The actor William Petersen – who never quite achieved the stardom this film seemed to augur – was, like Brad Pitt, blessed (or cursed) with an almost ethereal beauty, but here convincingly conveys the mental fragility and faltering equilibrium of damaged FBI man Will Graham, still attempting to recover psychologically from the bruising encounter with the terrifying Lecter (actually spelt 'Lecktor' in this first cinematic incarnation, bringing to mind the Soviet decoding machine in Ian Fleming's *From Russia with Love* [1963]). Set against the more actorly performances of Brian Cox and the towering Tom Noonan, Peterson is coaxed by Mann into underplaying his vulnerable, all-too-empathetic character, allowing the audience to read his fragility by the merest subtle flicker of expression; it is, in fact, something of master class in underplaying, and certainly the apogee of the actor's career -- his subsequent work in the TV series *CSI* (in which the actor was physically heavier, playing an intuitive character not a million miles away from Will Graham) gave Peterson far less challenging material to work with.

TWO MONSTERS

Tom Noonan's performance as the dangerously disturbed serial killer Francis Dollarhyde (whose bizarre teeth marks on his victims earn him the soubriquet from the FBI 'The Tooth Fairy') is a method-style accomplishment of some considerable subtlety. Inevitably (because of the exigencies of the plot) the character's introduction is withheld from the audience for a lengthy amount of the film's running time. Dollarhyde's jolting initial appearance with a stocking distorting his face is particularly unsettling, coming prior to the torture and incendiary death of a luckless (and, significantly, rude) reporter who falls into his clutches. And although the principal function of the Dollarhyde character (both within the Harris novel and this first screen adaptation; he is a more ambiguous character in the later version which retained the *Red Dragon* title) is calculated to inspire fear in the audience, Noonan and his director nevertheless manage to convey the remnants of humanity within this psychopathic monster, particularly in the scenes which demonstrate a growing sympathy between Dollarhyde and a blind female colleague (sensitively played by Joan Allen) with whom he sleeps. It might be argued that although she does not see Dollarhyde in the same grotesque light as we do – nor, for that matter, is she is able to see the sinister home movies he plays of his victims while he is in the room with her – their relationship is a highly unlikely one, but given verisimilitude by Noonan's performance and the customarily adroit Allen.

SAD SEXUAL ENCOUNTERS

Interestingly, the attraction between these characters and its aftermath echoes another desperately sad encounter between a serial killer and a woman who temporarily befriends (and sympathises with) him – that of Norman Bates and Marion Crane in *Psycho*. In both films, there is a suggestion that the woman is facilitating the killer's accessing of their latent humanity and *simpatico* and perhaps offering a glimpse of some kind of redemption – except, of course, that it is simply too late. Both women are doomed by these encounters. Michael Mann acceded to the suggestion (the actor's own) that Tom Noonan be isolated from the rest of the cast members (apart from Joan Allen, the only other actor with whom he has a lengthy scene) and this method approach appears to have worked in fleshing out one of the modern screen's most distinctive monsters. Interestingly, Dollarhyde's agenda – to synthesise a variety of elements (including visual motifs from the fine arts) to create something finished and evolved – might be said to be a metaphor of precisely the process that Michael Mann attempts with the variegated elements of his film.

However, the psychotic Dollarhyde, for all his grim fascination, is not able to match Harris' signature character in terms of sheer, fascinating monstrousness, not least because of Hannibal Lecter's coruscating intelligence and Sherlock Holmes-like powers of deduction. In *Red Dragon* (and *Manhunter*), Lecter remains behind bars for the duration of the narrative, although he acts as a menacing criminal *éminence grise*, putting both Will Graham (the man who caught him) and his family in danger. As this is the narrative structure that Michael Mann is obliged to work with (unless major surgery were to be performed on the original novel), it is a mark of the writer/director's achievement that in the limited amount of screen time allotted to Lecter, Mann ensures that the murderous psychiatrist's appearances are burned into the audience's consciousness.

A crucial tactic (captured by Dante Spinotti, in images of great purity) is the use of setting, such as the antiseptic white cell in which we first see Lecter behind both glass and bars. It is a colour scheme echoed in the entire institution, as we are subsequently to see when a claustrophobic Will Graham runs down winding corridors, hyperventilating after his unnerving encounter with his old nemesis. The spotless environment – and Lecter's own white prison garb – is the perfect counterpoint to the stygian darkness that we quickly learn is at the fulcrum of the man's psyche. Similarly, the secondary killer Dollarhyde's apartment – in the film's unsettling production design – has a powerful resonance as a dark, metaphor for his twisted, cluttered mentality.

THE FIRST LECTER

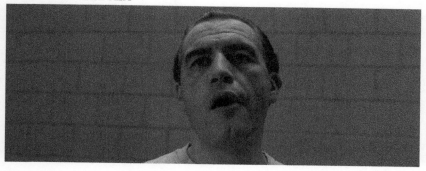

The first Lecter: Brian Cox as 'Lecktor' in Manhunter

But crucial to the success of the Lecter scenes is the actor chosen to incarnate this well-read, cultivated monster. In his most canny piece of casting, Mann's choice of the Scottish actor Brian Cox is a masterstroke (although it's interesting to speculate how other actors considered for the part – such as Brian Dennehy, Mandy Patinkin and John Lithgow – would have handled this initial screen incarnation).

An interesting syndrome has grown up around this first cinema version of Hannibal Lecter, not dissimilar to that which has followed the various screen versions of Henning Mankell's phlegmatic Swedish detective Kurt Wallander. While the performance by Kenneth Branagh in the role for the BBC's English language version has its adherents, it became *de rigueur* among Mankell aficionados to praise the Swedish actor Krister Henriksson's earlier incarnation of the role as more subtle and truthful, with a studied avoidance of 'actorliness'. Precisely the same syndrome has grown up around Brian Cox's performance of Lecter when contrasted with that of the Welsh Anthony Hopkins. Certainly Cox's performance is more understated, and in another documentary created for the DVD of *Manhunter*, the actor explained his decision to use an English accent for the role (as opposed to the subtle – and textually more accurate – American one utilised by Hopkins): Cox felt that Michael Mann, like himself, regarded evil as being more persuasive when emanating from a more European source (something of throwback to the worldly Europe vs. naive America polarity of the novels of Henry James). Mann suggested an English public school pupil as an exemplar – an accent that is mistrusted, apparently, by many Americans (or perhaps just by Michael Mann).

Certainly, the few minutes of screen time allotted to the actor in *Manhunter* are played in a style which, with the passage of time and many more notable screen appearances to his credit, we can now recognise as being not untypical of Brian Cox; his Lecktor/Lecter is laid-back, slightly avuncular and effectively amiable when dealing with his hated opponent Will Graham, the cruel mind games more lightly played than by Hopkins. The latter's approach to the role bespoke a barely-reined-in relish, allowing the glint of madness to surface in a more ostentatious fashion. But an examination of both actors in the role demonstrates that the critical truism that Cox was 'closer' to Harris's characters will simply not bear scrutiny. The subtle psychological attacks by Cox's character on the wary, treading-on-eggshells Will Graham do not possess the carefully orchestrated nuance of similar scenes in Jonathan Demme's film and the first encounter between the two is not as disturbing as that between Hopkins and Jodie Foster. Nevertheless, Cox utilises a quietly unsettling humour to good effect and his presence saturates the film, extending an influence far beyond the limited screen time he is allowed.

The Celtic background of the actors who have played Hannibal Lecter (excepting Gaspard Ulliel, who play the serial killer as a younger man in the nondescript *Hannibal Rising* [2007]), is most instructive in the sense that a certain balance was required: both Brian Cox and Anthony Hopkins are rarely called upon to utilise their Scottish and Welsh antecedents in their performances. Both actors are well aware that received pronunciation was *de rigueur* for the classical repertoire (along with, latterly, an ability to mimic the American accent when working in the US – which both men do faultlessly) and although it is Cox rather than Hopkins who utilises a British-sounding accent in his Lecter outing, both employ a well-spoken, crisp delivery that Americans traditionally associate with an English accent. It is interesting that Frankie Faison, who plays the psychiatric nurse Barney (and is the only actor to appear in four Hannibal Lecter films), when extolling the virtues of Hopkins' performance stresses its Englishness. But having said that, it is perhaps necessary to enter into the realms of stereotype and suggest that both Hopkins and Cox channel what might be considered a certain Celtic mischievousness or playfulness into their performances – and a fantasy mental recasting of the film with, say, Jeremy Irons in the role, would not lend itself to this version of Lecter's non-English strain of whimsy.

After the final bloody encounter between Graham and an operatically murderous Dollarhyde, we are offered the possibility that this time Graham may be able to heal the psychological scars of this encounter with more success than those left by his battle with Lecter, aided by the detective's loving wife and son. As for Lecter himself, his most memorable screen incarnation was yet to come, for a director not as crucially concerned with the visual style of his films, Jonathan Demme. But, in fact, as we shall see, Demme proved to be every bit as rigorous a director as his more flamboyant, style-conscious predecessor.

JONATHAN DEMME'S *THE SILENCE OF THE LAMBS*

Jonathan Demme (right) shares a joke with a muzzled Anthony Hopkins

To say that director Jonathan Demme's career has been chequered does not begin to do justice to a series of films that frequently bears the signature of a talented auteur but which, of late, appears to have been drained of all the things that once made his work so exhilarating and inventive. Like several other major American talents, his alma mater was the Roger Corman school of film-making, with the king of American exploitation movies giving him his first break. Unlike Francis Coppola, whose tyro venture for Corman was in in the horror field (the delirious, meaninglessly-titled *Dementia 13* in 1963), Demme was given crime film assignments with healthy doses of sex (*de rigueur* for the canny Corman): *Caged Heat* in 1974 and the lively and accomplished *Crazy Mama* two years later. After Corman, his first major venture in the thriller field was the taut, Hitchcockian *Last Embrace* in 1979, but his real identity as a film-maker began to emerge in a series of genuinely quixotic and unusual films such as *Melvin and Howard* (1980), *Swing Shift* (1984 – compromised by the proverbial 'artistic differences' with its star and producer, Goldie Hawn) and the frenetic (and at times surrealistic) *Something Wild* in 1986.

In terms of commercial success, *The Silence of the Lambs* five years later quickly assumed pole position in Demme's career, and established him as a master of the thriller form; but it was a field he quickly abandoned for the popular but meretricious (and lugubrious) AIDS drama *Philadelphia* in 1993 and the similarly worthy (and notably inert) *Beloved* in 1998, based on Toni Morrison's novel. Since the mid-1980s Demme has been a prolific documentarian, from concert films (such as *Stop Making Sense* [1984]) to political portraits (*Jimmy Carter: Man from Plains* [2007]), and it is arguably the case that these are now more representative of his body of work than the larger budget studio pictures he still occasionally helms. His return to the thriller with a remake of John Frankenheimer's classic *The Manchurian Candidate* (in 2004) was coolly received, and almost universally found to be wanting when compared to the matchless original, but there has been something of a revisionist upgrading of its reputation of late.

Like many an auteur (from Hitchcock to Bergman), Demme clearly feels comfortable surrounding himself with creative personnel that he has worked with repeatedly: cinematographer Tak Fujimoto, the composer Howard Shore, the sound mixer Chris Newman, the character actor Charles Napier, and others. But such is the panoply of subjects that he has tackled, even this familiar crew do not confer an air of uniformity on his films.

The opening sequence of *The Silence of the Lambs*, in which we see Clarice Starling running in a sweat suit through a sylvan forest, establishes in economical fashion several things about the character. First of all, of course, there is a certain level of physical fitness – she is able to deal with the variety of obstacles she encounters (including a rope climbing frame), although clearly does not find the activity quite as straightforward as an athlete would; some strain is evident. We also learn (as the sequence progresses) that Clarice is training on an FBI course, and is, in fact, a cadet in the Bureau, held in some esteem (despite her inexperience) by her quietly-spoken boss, Jack Crawford. We see her greet a fellow female colleague, a young black woman, Ardelia – the only friend on her own level we see her interact with during the course of the film. Summoned from the obstacle course even before she has time to shower (and is therefore at a disadvantage, bathed in sweat and hardly looking her best), Clarice is called to the office of her boss, a man we sense she respects and is (simultaneously) slightly intimidated by.

Odd one out? Clarice Starling (Jodie Foster) doesn't just have serial killers to overcome

Demme here includes a significant shot in which Clarice, catching the elevator, is surrounded male colleagues, introducing early on notions of gender and power which are to be examined throughout the film.

Certain elements in the original novel pertaining to the Jack Crawford character are wisely removed in the film adaptation, such as his anguished visits to the bedside of his dying wife. Although in the source material this is an important element, in the context of the filleting that is necessary when creating a screenplay from a novel, such peripheral elements not only become inessential, but their removal can forge a certain opaqueness which is actually helpful to a particular film (as when Clint Eastwood persuaded Sergio Leone to abandon acres of dialogue when the two worked together in Italy on the 'spaghetti Westerns'). Here, the streamlining obliges us to regard Crawford (to some degree) from the outside – in precisely the way, in fact, that Starling perceives him. We know no more about him than she does, and this mystique makes the character, and his motives regarding Starling, more intriguing.

This strip-mining of detail for cinematic purposes is in fact one of the signal achievements of the screenwriter Ted Tally, and it is an achievement that will be appreciable only by those familiar with the original novel. A comparison here might be drawn with the books (and subsequent films of) the popular thriller writer of an earlier generation, Alistair Maclean. Many of his later books began to read like treatments for the (inevitable) subsequent films, with all the essential elements shoe-horned in to facilitate the requisite number of set pieces.

PSYCH AND CRIMINOLOGY

Demme gives us the story of 'Bill' and his victims in one shot

On the cork board behind Crawford's head we see the *National Enquirer*-style tabloid headline 'Bill Skins Fifth', making it quickly apparent to us that a serial killer has become a major priority for the Bureau. Crawford makes it clear that Clarice is to be used in order to obtain information from the incarcerated serial killer Hannibal Lecter to help track down the murderous 'Buffalo Bill' – so called because he is removing part of the skin of his victims – before he claims more lives. The FBI is clearly worried about the lack of progress it is making in the case, and similarly, Clarice is conscious about her own personal progress within the Bureau. The opportunity she is offered is, therefore, distinctly advantageous (should it prove successful), for both her and her employers. Clarice has majored in Psych and Criminology at UVA, and has spent time as an intern at a psychiatric clinic, but this assignment is to represent her first engagement with serial killers.

We next see her, now a smartly dressed and capable looking individual, dealing with the unpleasant Dr Chilton, in charge of the Baltimore psychiatric prison in which Lecter is imprisoned. Chilton, who makes inappropriate advances to Clarice (which she politely but firmly sidesteps) gives his own assessment of why Crawford has chosen her for the assignment suggesting that her prettiness is to be used as a tool to 'turn on' Lecter (who, we are told, has not even seen a woman in eight years); Chilton remarks that Clarice will be very much to Lecter's murderous taste (just as she clearly is to the oleaginous Dr Chilton).

Of course, unpleasant though Chilton is, he can hardly match his appalling charge, who has eviscerated nine people and eaten the tongue of a prison nurse. Chilton boasts that Lecter regards him as his nemesis, and points out just how much hatred there is between the two men. This spleen will come to bear an ironic and gruesome fruit later in the film.

FINESSING THE AUDIENCE

The first appearance of Lecter in *The Silence of the Lambs* is prepared for by Demme and his team as assiduously as any of Shakespeare's great character entrances (and the psychiatrist shares certain characteristics with his famous forbears, such as a striking charisma – and an overweening self-regard). We have been introduced to the self-regarding, pompous Chilton, and it is here that the work of Demme's casting director Howard Feuer continues to show impeccable results. Anthony Heald, in the role, is supremely unpleasant. It might be argued that Demme and Feuer are colluding in Harris's finessing of sure-fire Pavlovian responses in his audience – in other words, the casting strategy shows that they are doing the best possible justice to the tactics utilised by Harris in the original novel. The very capable Heald has clearly been encouraged to be as unattractively oleaginous as possible, with gelled long hair that (in film shorthand) suggests untrustworthiness. By this point, we are already, of course, firmly locked in the consciousness of Clarice, so the doctor's supercilious manner and apparent contempt for his patients have already rendered him unsympathetic even before his crass attempts at asking Clarice out for a date are rebuffed – an early demonstration of the politeness that is to win Clarice some kudos with Hannibal Lecter (for whom courtesy is a cardinal virtue).

Few works of popular genre cinema have the time (or the interest) to explore the nuances of human behaviour and prefer to delineate such things in bright poster colours (film-makers generally subscribe to HL Mencken's dictum that nobody ever went broke underestimating the taste – or intelligence – of the public). But this is most certainly not the case with Jonathan Demme and Ted Tally, as evinced by their treatment of the unpleasant attempts at seduction of Clarice by Dr Chilton. Without ever over-stressing the change of attitude in the character when he realises that he will not get very far with his attractive visitor, we witness a sudden *froideur* in his dealings with her, and his true feelings (which are, it is suggested, of a misogynistic nature) become more apparent. This ties in with the perception of the film as having a progressive feminist agenda (which links it thematically with Demme's oeuvre), i.e. the suggestion that Starling's only interest for Chilton is in a libidinous sense; his apparent acknowledgement of her gifts is purely cosmetic – a means to a sexually self-interested end.

THE DEVIL IS IN THE DETAIL

The fact that *The Silence of the Lambs* is such an exemplary artefact of the screenwriter's craft may be underlined by the fact that there are actually few non-essential elements in the novel lending themselves to easy removal. The immense amount of novelistic detail in Harris's original is never there simply to provide texture (as per the facile instructions in a creative writing course) – such detail is always absolutely at the service of finessing elements of character and narrative development; the removal of such material, while *de rigueur* for the exigencies of fashioning a screenplay is no easy task, though Tally accomplishes it with understated skill. As mentioned earlier, in the universe of the film, we are no longer (as viewers) party to the consciousness of Jack Crawford, or (for that matter) the mindset and psyches of the two killers, Hannibal Lecter and Jame Gumb – or even, it might be argued, directly linked to the thought processes of Clarice Starling. But without the utilisation of a voiceover (a device that simply would not have worked in the game plan established here by the director, removing the shadings which the audience are allowed to fill in for themselves), what we are shown regarding the mental processes of the heroine by the nuances of Foster's performance and the subtle use of *mise en scène* to flesh out her character bring an almost novelistic richness to the character, and the removal of certain narrative components is always justified. What is always apparent is the determination of this young woman to make a mark in a man's world. And here, again, any feminist agenda is never bluntly formulated verbally – one of the many examples of an assumption of intelligence on the part of the viewer. It might be argued that Starling's need for the blandishments of a masculine authority figure (and the film contains two such, one positive and paternal, the other negative and almost vampiric) ensures that any doctrinaire feminist reading of the film is difficult to sustain. The complexity of Starling's response to Crawford is somewhat different in the film to that in the novel – in the latter, unaware of the conflict and worry in the FBI chief's character caused by his wife's illness, she interprets his unsettling changes of mood as a wavering response to her gender in terms of her suitability for the job. Once again, the streamlining of this element of the book is entirely to the film's advantage.

After Clarice is instructed by Chilton in the rigorous procedures necessary for any encounter with Lecter (further instilling apprehension in the audience), we are presented with the same antiseptic white walls for Lecter's place of incarceration that we had seen in *Manhunter*, but the effect here is not so theatrical (colour is used more naturalistically), and the institution accordingly has a touch more veracity. However, Clarice's tense walk along the dark corridor to Lecter's cell is more unsettling than that in the early film, with each cell containing a disturbed (and disturbing-looking) individual, the most unpleasant of whom is unquestionably the gibbering 'Multiple' Miggs, who approaches Clarice hoarsely whispering 'I can smell your cunt!' And while this obscenity tells the audience all we need to know about this murderous individual, Miggs' behaviour has a surprising corollary when it is later discussed by Clarice with Lecter. In terms of production design, the contrast of the 'house of horrors' corridor with the antiseptic cell at its end is vaguely surrealistic (and even expressionistic). The setting coveys both a possible (if unlikely) option for imprisoning extremely dangerous psychopaths, and is also – at least in Lecter's case – a visual representation of the killer's mind, with its Stygian horror film aspect: the dungeon-like corridors with sinister prisoners through which Clarice is obliged to pass (as if on a journey to an anteroom of hell) contrasted with its modern high-tech accoutrements when we finally reach the cell containing Lecter. It boasts a variety of technological devices which allow the psychiatrist a certain degree of diversion while severely restricting his freedom (for the purposes of protecting those who come into contact with this most dangerous of men).

There is perhaps an echo in this sequence of an earlier arcane mix of Gothic horror and modernistic settings: the bizarre *art nouveau* house of the Boris Karloff character in

Edgar Ulmer's cult film *The Black Cat* (1934; interestingly, also a film which features the skinning of human bodies, handled with a degree of restraint equal to that employed by Demme). But whereas the futuristic setting of the Ulmer film (from his own sketches) is impossible to ignore, an audience might not notice the intriguing mix of styles in Demme's prison complex.

The synthesis of elements that create the look and identity of a film come from a variety of talents: from the director's original conception, to the cinematographer's realisation of the same; to the production designer. In the case of *The Silence of the Lambs*, these three elements are in perfect harmony, producing a visual signature for the film which is highly distinctive and very specific to Demme's vision (different directors have not attempted to replicate the visual style of Demme and co. for later Hannibal Lecter outings). Such elements as the released moths that are given free rein in Jame Gumb's/Buffalo Bill's squalid kitchen suggest an environment in which something is subtly wrong. Kristi Zea, the highly accomplished production designer, creates a contrast between very disparate settings: Lecter's cell, the training ground at the FBI, the oak-panelled courtroom in which Lecter is temporarily incarcerated and the final menace-laden lair of the film's on-the-loose killer Gumb. And while all these settings are brimming with carefully observed detail (not to mention the sharply observed small-town America with its blue-collar industrial environments) the real achievement of Zea is perhaps one that is not immediately apparent on the first (or even subsequent) viewings of the film – that is to say, creating a cohesive universe against which Thomas Harris's characters can act out their disturbing scenarios without ever suggesting a lurch from one level of reality to the next. Even Gumb's house – the nearest the film comes to Daniel Haller's gothic production design for Roger Corman's Edgar Allan Poe adaptations – though somewhat over the top (notably with its sunken pit in which the luckless, filthy victims are imprisoned), remains basically grounded in a kind of reality (note the grease-encrusted stove on which Gumb prepares his meals – and possibly uses for more sinister processing purposes).

THE FIRST MEETING

Lecter 2.0: our first sight of Anthony Hopkins

The initial meeting between Clarice Starling and the murderous psychiatrist Hannibal Lecter is one of the great set pieces of modern cinema, justly celebrated, frequently imitated and parodied. While clearly adhering to the imperatives of poplar cinema, the sequence is shot and acted with a rigour worthy of the 'chamber cinema' of the Swedish master Ingmar Bergman in his late 1960s films such as *Persona* (1966) — and this is not the only occasion in which the more rarefied agendas of art cinema are evoked by Demme and his collaborators. As Clarice has made her way past the sinister cellmates who inhabit the same block as Lecter, first time audiences were disarmed by their first sight of a monster for who they might have thought they had been well prepared. They may have been expecting an overtly sinister figure, or perhaps a crabbed, sepulchral one, bound to be physically repulsive in the extreme. The first sight of the actor Anthony Hopkins standing upright and alert in a boiler suit with a fixed smile on his handsome face, short hair neatly slicked back, is the absolute opposite of what audiences have been led to expect given the variety of warnings impressed upon Clarice and the viciousness of Lecter's crimes. Surely, we think, this not unattractive (if unsettling) figure cannot be the monster we have heard about? The initial response of audiences in 1991 to Hopkins' first appearance was sometimes a gasp or a snort of laughter — not of derision, but a wry realisation of our own readiness to be led up the garden path and be presented with the last thing we expected — the sight of a charismatic actor. Inevitably, of course, comparisons must be made with the first appearance of Brian Cox in *Manhunter*, and for all the considerable virtues of the earlier actor's incarnation of the role, there is an added element here, a dramaturgical consolidation of Hopkins' performance which Michael Mann did not accord Cox.

Very quickly, Jonathan Demme and his cinematographer Tak Fujimoto establish an almost musical counterpoint in the juxtaposition of close shots of his two actors, and it is this piece of subtly utilised technique which (as much as anything else) renders the scene so effective. Firstly, of course, there is the writing, with Ted Tally's screenplay utilising many of the perfectly judged lines from the Harris novel (why try to improve on an element which needed no burnishing?), along with the cannily judged acting which mixed a certain degree of larger-than-life, indicative characterisation on the part of Hopkins (unquestionably the apposite choice for the character's introduction) set against the vulnerable, walking-on-eggshells performance given by Foster, in which the performance effects are far more inconspicuously sketched in: delicate charcoal strokes as opposed to the broad-brush poster colour mode adapted by Hopkins. But if this suggests an antimony between two acting styles which refuse to gel, nothing could be further from the truth: both actors are clearly interested in the interior lives of the characters and incorporate much nuance and shading into the most inconspicuous details: a sudden opacity of expression alternates abruptly with a laser-like intensity in both actors. It should also be noted that Demme is well aware of the charismatic qualities of his performers and utilises such elements in quite a self-conscious fashion, inviting us to judge the physical appeal of his actors. Over the years, Hopkins has frequently demonstrated what appears to be a genuine bemusement at the fact that he is considered attractive (describing himself as a 'short-arsed Welshman'), but Jonathan Demme is well aware that Hopkins' self-deprecating assessment is very far from the truth, and showcases a mesmeric performance that focuses on Hopkins' piercing eyes.

For the duration of the interview, the audience is on tenterhooks for the vulnerable, ill-at-ease Clarice, who is clearly no match for the immensely manipulative (and immensely polite – except when he chooses not to be) Lecter. It is clear to us that she is bearing in mind Jack Crawford's firm dictum (repeated by the odious Chilton) that it would be a mistake to impart any personal information to the imprisoned man ('Believe me, you don't want Hannibal Lecter inside your head'). Needless to say, Lecter is soon employing subtle, Machiavellian tactics to circumvent these warning systems, and we are relieved when Clarice is able to stay just about one jump ahead of Lecter (using the tactic of never explicitly replying to him when he makes his searching personal queries).

FORENSIC EXAMINATION

As the two very different individuals uneasily converse (mostly in close-up), we find ourselves examining the contents of Lecter's cell with quite as much intense forensic attention as the young FBI agent shows (we are later to learn that she has not missed a single facet of the cell), and it is clear that the reined-in, quietly-spoken Lecter is a very different kettle of fish to the deranged or catatonic-looking individuals in the other cells. There are the visible signs of the psychiatrist's cultured artistic personality: drawings of the city of Florence (drawings, in fact, by Lecter himself – and that historic Italian city with its famous art galleries is to figure in subsequent chapters of the Hannibal story, both books and films); we are to learn of the man's love of the music of Bach (the *Goldberg Variations* for keyboard features prominently in a gruesome later sequence), and there are other books suggesting his intelligence and knowledge of the humanities (ironic, given the psychiatrist's own spectacular inhumanity). On Lecter's shelves – in a blackly comic touch – is a book on cooking; we remember Clarice's almost-whispered response on hearing Jack Crawford intone his name: 'Hannibal the cannibal.' And this initial interrogation scene is, of course, the one in which Hopkins delivers what has become one of the most memorable lines in the history of film: Hannibal's devouring of a hapless census taker's liver with 'a nice Chianti and some Fava beans', delivered with the bizarre 'slurping' sounds Hopkins makes with his lips, as chilling (and, simultaneously, hilarious) as any of the film's copious, graphic bloodletting (the 'lip-smacking' notion was, in fact, the actor's, enthusiastically welcomed by the director). We quickly become aware of the doctor's immense self-regard and ruthlessly-applied rules of conduct as rigorous as anything to be found in a theocratic country – it is this, combined with his old-world courtesy, that we must set against the knowledge that Lecter is a brutal psychopath. There is a private class war between the patrician Lecter and his younger, ex-blue-collar interlocutor; the once-respectable, professional Lecter attempts to score points by displaying his upper-middle-class contempt for the trailer trash ethos that produced Clarice, and we fear for her – particularly when she seems to be on the point of being tempted into making an ill-advised revelation. And we are uneasily aware that (almost certainly) the quid pro quo Lecter demands for his co-operation will be enacted before the narrative is over, and that Clarice will be obliged to make some kind of revealing self-admission. (What we do not know at this point is that her key admission will explain the significance of the film's cryptic title.)

Lecter has made it clear that the one thing he requires after eight years in his cell is a view. He is well aware that he will never be let out while he is alive, but it is his keenest wish to be far away from Dr Chilton, and for that he is prepared to offer Clarice the thing she needs – a psychological profile of the psychopathic Buffalo Bill based on the case evidence. He will, he says, help Claris catch her prey.

CHARACTER ANALYSIS

Those viewers who admire *The Silence of the Lambs* are wont to relate their favourite moments in the film, be they of acting, writing or direction (such is the well-crafted distinction on offer in all these areas). But a particularly choice sequence, much admired by aficionados, is a perfect concatenation of all three elements, in which Lecter makes his devastating (and cruel) character analysis of Clarice Starling – an analysis which provides us, the viewer, with new information. It is information that we are not necessarily party to, but accept to be the truth – much in the same fashion that we admire and accept the astonishing deductions of Sherlock Holmes (very much the exemplar for the sequence). Anthony Hopkins, in a beautifully underplayed sotto voce delivery, says:

> You're so ambitious, aren't you? You know what you look like to me, with your good bag and your cheap shoes? You look like a rube. A well-scrubbed, hustling rube with a little taste. Good nutrition has given you some length of bone, but you're not more than one generation from poor white trash, are you, Agent Starling? And oh, how quickly the boys found you! All those tedious, sticky fumblings, in the back seats of

cars, while you could only dream of getting out. Getting anywhere... getting all the way to the F...B... I.

Such dialogue, of course, is a gift to any actor, but it is difficult to imagine it being delivered with more understated relish than Hopkins utilises here. The sequence adds texture to both characters in the context of the narrative (we read Clarice's uncomfortable response to this analysis with great attention, tempted, against our more generous natures, to indulge in a certain *schadenfreude* at her expense), and grants a level of personality nuance alien to most popular commercial products – such as (we should not forget) Demme's film essentially remains. Lecter has also revealed himself (unsurprisingly) as a snob; he is not only Clarice's intellectual superior but also her social superior – and he can't resist the pleasure of putting her in her place. Class is, in fact, a key theme of the film.

RIDDLE ME THIS

After Lecter has lost patience with Starling's careful but obvious attempts to inveigle information out of him, he brusquely rebuffs her offer, and she leaves. But after Miggs flicks his semen into her face, Lecter urgently calls her back, appalled at the behaviour of his fellow inmate. Miggs has committed the worst sin in Lecter's eyes, that of discourtesy. It is this which has finally prompted him to assist her in what she loves most – advancement. He says to her, 'Look deep within yourself', and tells her to seek out an old patient, a Miss Hester Mofet, spelling out the name 'M. O. F. E. T.'. These, in fact, are riddles, and (after deciphering) are to lead Starling to a horrifying discovery in a lock-up.

Before this discovery, however, we are shown Starling back at work (and making mistakes) in the FBI training facility; we are reminded that she is no super-capable fighting machine along the lines of Stieg Larsson's Lisbeth Salander, as the tyro agent is outmanoeuvred by one of her trainers in an exercise involving guns. Most film audiences are (to varying degrees) cine-literate, and even those unfamiliar with the source novel will have realised that this scene represents a canny placing of important information which will become relevant for another sequence later in the film. It is this strategy (i.e. orchestration of delayed effects) which is a *sine qua non* of the work of the director

Alfred Hitchcock, whose techniques were clearly part of Jonathan Demme's cinematic DNA when making his film. In the final, clammy sequence of *The Silence of the Lambs*, Starling will be placed in a situation where her knowledge of her own 'danger areas' is crucial to her survival.

Called to her second meeting with Jack Crawford, she is informed that the appalling Miggs is dead – he has swallowed his own tongue. Crawford informs her that Lecter has done it to amuse himself, but we are aware that the real reason for the death is the transgression of manners by Miggs which it is so important to Lecter – and without any visualisation of the scene, it is once again imparted to the viewer just what a dangerous opponent Lecter can be. Crawford asks about the name that was given to her – Mofet – but the key to riddle is as much Lecter's use of the word 'yourself' as well as the anagram of the name he mentions – 'Hester Mofet' is 'the rest of me'. But she has tracked down – and is to venture into – a self storage facility outside of downtown Baltimore, a unit pre-paid ten years earlier with a contract in the name of Hester Mofet.

SET PIECE TWO

In another of the film's adroit set pieces, we follow Starling to a lock-up/garage to investigate the lead she has obtained from Lecter. It is dark, and the weather is inclement. Access to the storage facility is virtually impossible, and the owner is not prepared to help her open the unit – once again it is Starling's ability to improvise which allows her to continue her investigation by penetrating the lock-up. The exploration of the deeply sinister enclosed area – with a gruesome discovery at the end of the search – is a reminder (if such a reminder were required) that both the novel and the film are firmly located within the nerve-jangling territory of the horror genre, in which the steady orchestration of suspense and the delivery of deferred, gruesome revelations are key elements. Those who know Demme's film only from an acquaintance with a DVD viewing on a domestic television screen will be unaware of just how effectively this scene works in unsettling the viewer in the cinema, but this is not just on the level of the mechanics of suspense; the investigation of the darker recesses of the human psyche is a metaphor here, and it is as strongly worked out as any such impulse is in the film.

The discovery of a human head in a jar is a concrete example of exactly what horrific areas the film is prepared to take the audience to. (I will return to this scene in 'Making Horror Respectable'.)

THE SECOND INTERVIEW

In Clarice Starling's second interview with Hannibal Lecter there is a distinctly different dynamic to that found in their first meeting. Apart from the fact that Starling has had her own personal demonstration of the lethal power of her interlocutor by the death of his demented cellmate, she has also been led by Lecter to the discovery of a severed human head. The sober warnings she was given about the psychiatrist have been proven to be – if anything – an understatement of his capabilities. But this second interrogation is also played in a subtly different manner to that of its earlier counterpart. While the power base between the two characters has shifted slightly, Lecter remains very much a chess grandmaster, affecting canny moves which are initially unclear to his opponent, but the viewer senses a growing degree of respect on the murderer's part towards Starling. Here again, it is as much the playing of the two principals, Foster and Hopkins, full of subtle gradations of tone, which allows the alert viewer to observe that both characters are aware of – and exploring -- the infinitesimal shifts in their relationship. Hopkins remains as playful as ever (with the ever-present streak of the malign), but Foster conveys an awareness that she does, to some degree, now command a modicum of respect which was hardly apparent in their first meeting. We are inevitably reminded of her vulnerability (she has come straight from the lock-up and is rain- and sweat-drenched), and Lecter is to take her into extremely painful areas in his continuing game of quid pro quo as the duo exchange information.

As Starling asks whose head was in the bottle, Lecter counters with: 'Why don't you ask me about Buffalo Bill?' She asks if he knows anything about his successor in the serial killing field, and Lecter replies that he might – if he were to have access to the case files. But he is prepared to talk about 'Miss Mofet', whose real name was Benjamin Raspail and was in fact a former patient of the Doctor's ('His romantic attachments ran to, shall we say, the exotic...', Lecter confides). To both Clarice and our surprise, he informs her that he did not kill his ex-patient, but merely 'tucked him away', much as he found him. Starling, obviously sceptical, asks if not Lecter himself, then who did kill him? The psychiatrist's answer is typically playful (and horrifying): 'Who can say? Best thing for him, really. His therapy was going nowhere. His dress, make up...'

SLEIGHT-OF-HAND

At this point, we once again we find ourselves surprised by the legerdemain that Demme extrapolates so successfully from the Harris novel. Lecter abruptly changes the conversation to a discussion of Jack Crawford and his interest in Clarice Starling. If audiences really examined Lecter's insights (of which this is a classic example), they might be bemused by (or sceptical of) the fact that this incarcerated prisoner can have access to so much privileged information. But the conjuring trick played by director and screenwriter in such instances is to maintain the level of focused intensity that simply steers us away from such inconvenient questions. Lecter attempts to embarrass Starling again with sexually explicit questions: 'Do think Jack Crawford wants you, sexually? True, he is much older, but do you think he visualises scenarios, exchanges, fucking you?'

Her reply to this deliberately provocative sortie demonstrates the quiet assurance Clarice is now able to call upon in her dealings with Lecter, and the neutral delivery by Foster points up the lines in the most apposite fashion: 'That doesn't interest me and, frankly, it's a sort of thing that Miggs would say.' But just as we are thinking that this is the most cutting rejoinder that Starling could make, comparing Lecter to a fellow patient he despised, Hopkins, with equally quiet understatement, replies: 'Not any more.'

BUFFALO BILL AT WORK

In another sharply-etched suspense sequence, we see Buffalo Bill (who we are now able to examine at length) abduct a plump young woman (his targets are customarily overweight females) who, we are to learn, is Catherine Martin, the daughter of United States Senator Ruth Martin. It is the kind of queasy and unnerving sequence that cannot fail to have the viewer fervently wishing that the victim will not be taken in by the subterfuge being used on her (helping Bill load a couch onto a van) – but knowing that she will be. The modus operandi of Buffalo Bill is constructed by Harris (and reproduced in the film) with a plausibility that is both persuasive and chilling. Starling is to learn from his file that he has claimed five victims (at least, five victims whose bodies have been discovered). After kidnapping the women, he keeps them alive for a short period before murdering them. Their bodies are then flayed before being thrown into the river. But the state of each victim's body is different – no two killings are exactly alike.

Starling accompanies Jack Crawford from the FBI camp at Quantico to West Virginia to examine the body of another of Buffalo Bill's victims which has recently been discovered. (The dialogue at this point is flat and unemotional: 'He keeps them alive for three days. We don't know why. No evidence of rape or physical abuse prior to death. All the mutilation you see is post-mortem.')

Again, Crawford gently tests Starling's ability to analyse what she knows of the killer they are both pursuing – a reminder that the whole narrative might be seen as something of an educational primer detailing the development/upskilling of Clarice Starling. She replies to her boss with a series of crisp deductions: the killer is a white male, as serial killers generally hunt within their own ethnic groups. She notes that the killer is in his thirties or forties, and has his own house, which is not an apartment. When asked why this is so, she points out that what he does requires privacy – and that, further, he is never impulsive.

One of the tactics utilised throughout the film is the steady parcelling out of information – for the benefit of both the characters and the audience – at precisely the moments were it becomes apropos. The accretion of story detail is handled both judiciously and in measured fashion. At this point, for the first time, Starling and Crawford discuss the real reason why she had been sent to interrogate Lecter – and, crucially, why she was not given a specific agenda prior to the first meeting. Crawford replies: 'If I'd sent you in with an actual agenda, Lecter would have known it instantly. He would have toyed with you and then turned to stone.'

LESS IS MORE

Clarice stands her ground and takes charge

The discretion with which the subsequent autopsy scene involving Bill's victim is handled is instructive when viewed from a distance of over two decades, and perhaps lends some credence to the much-repeated (and contentious) dictum that 'less is more'. In American television series featuring forensic pathologists (such as *CSI*, the programme on which *Manhunter*'s Will Graham, the actor William Petersen, continued his onscreen investigative career) and their British equivalents, the dispassionate autopsy scene is now almost *de rigueur*, and the tactics employed are now standard. Audiences once gasped at the realism with which horror film special effects technicians such as Carlo Rambaldi created queasily convincing simulacra of mutilated human bodies, but such effects are now quotidian, with the actors' dissection of convincingly gruesome body parts par for the course. In *The Silence of the Lambs*, Demme chooses to shoot his autopsy scene with a degree of discretion (at least in the opening moments), utilising the characters' responses to their macabre duty to unsettle the audience. Because the viewer is not party to the slicing of muscle and vein, we are allowed to mentally fill in precisely what is happening – the tactics, in effect, which were once necessary for censorship reasons, but which have subsequently fallen from favour. But it is another mark of the director's keen awareness of the ways in which he can work on the sensibilities of the audience that the first real view we are given of the dead girl is when her body is turned over and we see the hideous lesions and the swelling of the corpse that has taken place after the death.

TS Eliot famously said of the playwright John Webster that he 'saw the skull beneath the skin', and this sequence may be read as a similar examination of just what death does to the human body – the dissolution, in effect, that awaits us all. It is impossible not to consider one's own mortality while watching what is essentially a horror film set-piece.

Starling demonstrates her grasp of psychology by the judicious way in which she dismisses the policemen congregated in in the morgue before the autopsy. Their masculinity is an issue here, the viewer allowed to experience their impassive (but implicitly judgmental) stare from Starling's viewpoint in a 360 degree shot, echoing Crawford's rather cruel exclusion of her from his private conversation with the local sheriff. Casual, unthinking sexism is the hallmark of most of Starling's interactions with males through the film – the thin end of a wedge, it is implied, at the far end of which lies Buffalo Bill's murderous misogyny.

Again, there is a demonstration of Starling's acute powers of observation in examination of the body of the dead girl. She notes that two of the girl's nails are broken off and that she appears to have tried to claw her way through something. What follows is one of the most disturbing moments in the film, a sequence that still has the power to unsettle even after the many – and considerably more explicitly gruesome – films that have followed in the intervening years. Starling notices that the dead girl has something in her throat. It is a bug cocoon, so positioned that it could not have found its way into the dead girl's throat accidentally. The removal of the object is difficult to watch, and its significance will become apparent later in the film.

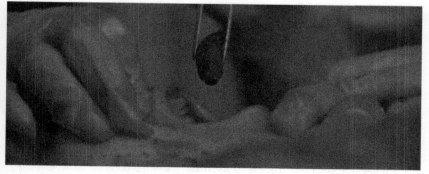

The first clue to 'Bill's' real motivation

Subsequent examination of this macabre find takes place with a colleague whose attraction for Starling is handled very differently in the original novel – any suggestion of a possible relationship at this point is expunged from the film (although he briefly reappears at the end of the film, suggesting that Starling draws a clear demarcation between work and personal life). It is revealed that the object is an Archerontia Styx – a Death's-head moth. Such insects only live in Asia, she is informed, and would have to have been raised in the United States from imported eggs – the creature was grown in America.

As news of the kidnapping of the senator's daughter gets out, Crawford authorises Clarice to present Lecter with a deal (one which, in fact, has no substance, although we do not know this yet and it remains unclear as to whether Starling does or not), offering him a prisoner transfer to a more attractive location if he will provide information that helps with the capture of Buffalo Bill and leads to the recovery of Catherine Martin. The bluff is an ill-advised move, and one which will have unfortunate consequences, but in her latest exchange with Lecter, Clarice is obliged to provide the most painful quid pro quo yet. And the performance by Jodie Foster – in a scene in which she reveals the significance of the title – is arguably the most subtle and carefully shaded moment that the actor brings to the film.

QUID PRO QUO

While the final interview (before his escape) between Clarice and Hannibal may inevitably lack the frisson of the duo's first edgy encounter, it is equally important in narrative terms, particularly so in the light of the revelations that are made about the young FBI investigator's personality painfully drawn out by her psychopathic interlocutor in this and their penultimate encounter. The setting, too, is markedly different from the antiseptic glass-walled cell at the institution where she first met him: he is now in a specially constructed cell in the centre of the hall of a local Tennessee courthouse, with a tall, box-like construction of bars contrasting with the oak panelling of the courthouse. Given the elaborate precautions regarding Lecter (the nigh-impregnable conditions of that first cell and the bizarre trussing-up and masking inflicted upon Lecter when he is

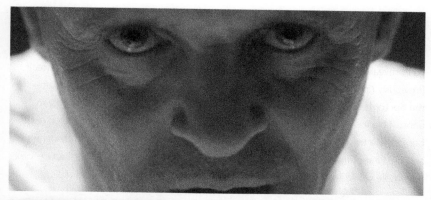

The close-ups in the scenes between Lecter and Starling become increasingly extreme, mirroring their intensity

transported), this final cell looks more permeable and our knowledge and expectations regarding the character's almost superhuman abilities make it look very fragile. The hockey mask worn by Lecter when in transit to Tennessee is significant in terms of binding the film's iconography to that of the horror genre, inevitably recalling the similar mask worn by the psychopathic (and unkillable) Jason Voorhees in the *Friday the 13th* franchise.

When Starling asks why the doctor has given false and misleading information to the senator so desperate to find her daughter, he remains implacable and continues the game of 'quid pro quo' that he had initiated earlier before he agreed to confide any information. Lecter insists that she complete her story regarding her worst childhood memory. The first revelation that she makes initially appears to be the furthest she could go in revealing the truth about herself, but we are to learn something more traumatic. Previously (in Baltimore), Clarice had told Lecter about the death of her father, after the doctor had instructed her not to lie about any detail, or he would know (it's an unprovable assertion that we – and Clarice – believe). She had quietly explained how her father, a town marshal, was fatally wounded on discovering a burglary in progress and died a month later: 'My mother died when I was very young. My father had become the whole world to me, and when he left me I had nothing. I was 10 years old.'

As so often in the film, Jodie Foster seems to create a direct line to the vulnerable psyche of her character here, where the subtle, understated delivery of these memories (palpably painful in the fashion in which they are wrenched from her) points up how far the character is from being a real match for the implacable Lecter. At this point, viewers of the film (and readers of the original novel) will not have seen the true minatory significance of the observation that follows from Lecter: 'You're very frank, Clarice. I think it would be quite something to know you in private life.'

Thomas Harris has been notably closemouthed about the game plan he had for his principal characters, and given the future developments (embryonic as yet) of the relationship between Clarice and Lecter, this remark, when viewing the film in the light of the subsequent novels and the films made from them, now has a striking and unpleasant resonance.

'Quid pro quo,' Clarice reminds Lecter of their bargain; for this confidence, he makes it clear that he knows that Buffalo Bill's victims were overweight ('So tell me about Miss West Virginia. Was she large? Big through the hips?'). Lecter also reveals that he had knowledge of something which had not yet been made public, and reiterates (in a passage that is both poetic and disturbing) the theme of the earlier outing for Lecter, *Red Dragon/Manhunter*: the notion of transformation. The rigour with which this theme is worked out during the course of the film (and, for that matter, throughout the Harris oeuvre) is notable here, as perhaps the most important transformation in the film is that involving Starling, moving tentatively from someone recognised for a certain talent but burdened by inexperience and insecurity, into the capable protagonist who is finally able to track the Minotaur in its lair and defeat it.

EM Forster's famous (and contentious) criticism of several Dickens characters in *Aspects of the Novel* – that these characters did not develop but simply reappeared and performed variations of actions that they had done previously – might be laid at the door of Harris in his creation of Hannibal Lecter. But a defence of Harris might be mounted from the point of view that the character of Lecter is so strong and fully-formed it does not require any development against that necessary for the Starling character.

METAMORPHOSIS

In his courthouse cell, Lecter expatiates on the significance of the moth discovered in the throat of Buffalo Bill's female victim when Clarice asked why he places them there. 'The significance of the moth is change,' intones Lecter. 'Caterpillar into chrysalis or pupa. And from thence into beauty. Our Billy wants to change too.' When Clarice points out that there is no correlation between transsexualism and violence, and that transsexuals are generally very passive (more information gleaned by Harris in his research into psychotherapy), Lecter again compliments her on her intelligence. He points out that she is now very close to the way she is going to catch her quarry, but – he makes it clear – he will require the dispensing of more information of a personal nature from Clarice, and audiences are now about to learn the significance of the cryptic title of the film.

For Jodie Foster, this is clearly the most significant scene in the film, and the one which will most test her mettle as an actress. Any attempt to give the lines she is to deliver an over-accentuated, 'actorly' value would undoubtedly have rendered them untruthful, and it is to the actress's credit (and to that of her director) that she renders precisely the attenuation and modulation of her voice that is required for this crucial revelation. Foster is able to convey the inner life of the character with maximum verisimilitude. Quietly, she talks about living with cousins on a sheep and horse ranch in Montana, and subsequently running away one night, having woken up unexpectedly. She tells him that she had crept up to the barn where she had heard 'some kind of screaming'. Lecter asks what she saw. 'Lambs,' she replies. 'They were screaming. They were slaughtering the spring lambs and they were screaming.' Unable to disperse the terrified animals, Clarice describes how she grabbed one lamb and fled the scene.

In writing less sophisticated than that of Thomas Harris and in the hands of a film-maker less accomplished than Jonathan Demme, this dialogue may well have seemed awkwardly tendentious and forced in its use of metaphor – the lambs, of course, that Clarice is so anxious to liberate from their fate, represent the various young women she attempts to save during the course of the film (one specific victim – the senator's daughter – and potential future victims of Buffalo Bill). The fact that she was so unsuccessful at her first attempt at saving those about to die (the animals) is the Damoclean sword that will hang over her during the course of the narrative. But such is the skill of writer, director and players that this revelation has a kind of gentle beauty, all the more striking within the macabre context within which it is set. It is a revelation that is to charge the rest of the film and allow us to review the preceding narrative with a greater understanding and depth.

Waking up in the dark to hear the awful screaming of the lambs is the nightmare that (Lecter speculates) will never leave Clarice. His reading of her psychology is that if she is able to save the imprisoned, tormented Catherine she will make them stop. But despite this lacerating admission, the meeting with Lecter is inconclusive, and this most frank of confidences does not buy Starling the information that she seeks – at least not yet; nothing is ever easy with Lecter. By this point in the film, viewers will realise that a carefully ordered strategy is being played out, and that we must be patient enough to allow the various pieces of the puzzle to fall into place at the allotted time. At the same time we realise that Clarice Starling does not possess the luxury of time and patience, and that a young woman's life (and if she survives, her sanity) is at stake, placed in deeper danger by the minute because of Hannibal Lecter's recalcitrance and preference for elaborate, precious mind games.

HORROR FILM STRATEGIES

Later on the same evening after Starling's inconclusive visit, Lecter effects an ingenious escape from his cell which does delineate the astonishing mental acuity of the psychiatrist and (in narrative terms) delivers a twist revelation of the kind that the French writers Pierre Boileau and Thomas Narcejac practised in such influential books as *D'entre les Morts* (1954) and *Celle qui n'était plus* (1955) (adapted for the cinema as *Vertigo* [1958] and *Les Diaboliques* [1955], respectively) – an audacious double-bluff which had audiences gasping at both its cleverness and its grisliness and wondering why they had allowed themselves to be taken in by the sleight-of-hand on display.

Those prepared to ignore the horror film credentials and accoutrements of *The Silence of the Lambs* (including, surprisingly, the straitlaced Academy Awards committee) are turning a blind eye to a sequence which in its sheer blood-drenched gruesomeness locates the film firmly in the horror film universe. As before in the film, in order to produce the requisite frisson of the macabre, Jonathan Demme utilises a judicial mix of the indirect (including a grossly eviscerated body which is never seen clearly and, accordingly, works in a disquieting fashion on the viewer's mind) and the spectacularly graphic – in which a human face, already cut away from its owner, is peeled off another face like a latex mask.

Local police and SWAT teams arrive at the building housing Lecter's cell to discover one apparently grotesquely injured guard barely clinging on to life while another has been disemboweled and fixed high on the iron bars of Lecter's cell, his limbs spread out in an image that strikingly recalls one of William Blake's strange and disturbing drawings (there is, of course, a Blake link in *Red Dragon*). It is this grim effect that Demme allows the viewer to see only peripherally; wisely, perhaps as even with this discreet treatment, it is fairly apparent to the modern viewer that the mutilated monstrosity on the bars is not really convincing as a human figure as much as an impressive prosthetic invention. Nevertheless, it was an image that had audiences gasping in the cinemas at the time of the film's release, and is certainly something of a *coup de theatre* – but not as memorably gruesome as that which is to follow shortly in an ambulance.

The disembowelled guard is played by the late Charles Napier, who had previously worked with the director on a number of occasions; a lantern-jawed character actor specialising in repellent and violent roles, thus superficially suitable grist to Lecter's mill. But Demme undercuts the audience's expectations of Lecter's gaolers; Napier may look like a typical movie hard case but here he is polite to Clarice and as courteous to Lecter as the circumstances allow. Both officers are just doing their jobs. Their premeditated and calmly despatched executions might be necessary for Lecter's escape but they give the lie to the argument that he only kills boring or rude people. Arguably more 'deserving' (in Lecter's terms) versions of this breed of marked-for-death character will appear again in subsequent films, such as the avaricious Italian police Inspector Pazzi in *Hannibal*.

What follows is an action sequence that is an almost text-book example of audience manipulation on an operatic scale, with Demme relishing his authoritative use of all the discrete elements of cinema; from ingenuity of narrative to kinetic cutting which seems to ignore sequential unity, to gruesome make-up effects and performance – the latter writ larger here than throughout the rest of the film.

The injured guard lies groaning on the floor, his mangled face looking like chopped meat, apparently the victim of one of Lecter's frenzied assaults. But as paramedics transport the surviving guard in an ambulance (and a SWAT team examines every inch of the building for Lecter, who has not been found), we come to the proficiently-handled double twist that was one of the talking points of the film on its original release (it goes without saying that an assumption in this study will be made that the reader is familiar with the film – and will not be nonplussed when revelations are discussed). The SWAT team finds a bloodied body in the elevator shaft, wearing Lecter's clothes. The search is over – or is it? Demme cuts back to the ambulance and the (presumably) mortally wounded guard suddenly sits up, swiftly (and horrifically) peeling off his 'face'. We realise that this is Lecter, wearing the flayed features of the guard that he killed (the body in the lift shaft, we now realise). But the luckless paramedics in the ambulance are soon to follow suit (off-camera), and the lethal Lecter is now on the loose, establishing a very different dynamic in this film from that Michael Mann was obliged to work with in *Manhunter*, with Lecter remaining incarcerated for the entire length of the narrative. In a film full of carefully spaced horrific moments, this bloody removal of a human face

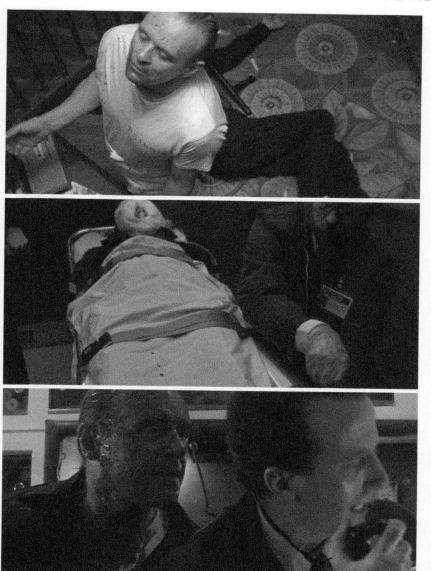

Lecter's escape: a heady concoction of violence, montage and misdirection

remains the most chilling on a sheerly visceral level, and places the film firmly in line with such famous (and notorious) horror opuses as Tobe Hooper's *The Texas Chain Saw Massacre* (1974, in which human faces, ripped from murder victims, are worn by their psychopathic killers). Howard Shore's score exacerbates the unease in disturbing and plangent fashion here.

It's instructive to compare the rarefied Hannibal Lecter with Hooper's obese redneck murderer, Leatherface. Indeed, most of the serial killers who have enjoyed repeated appearances in the cinema are markedly lower down the social scale than the cultivated, art-loving Lecter. Michael Myers from John Carpenter's *Halloween* (1978) is a lower-middle-class small town killer with no particular signs of education; the mutilated Freddie Kruger, created by academic turned horror director Wes Craven for *A Nightmare on Elm Street* (1984), was a working Joe (a school janitor) and a paedophile (an important characteristic and plot point in the first film that was abandoned when the striped-sweatered killer proved durable enough to sustain a lengthy sequence of films, not to mention child-friendly merchandise). But quite the most bottom-feeding of such movie killers is Hooper's dungaree-wearing, hammer-wielding farmer Leatherface.

Apart from simply being what one might describe (in pre-politically correct days) as poor white trash, the family of murderers and cannibals showcased in *The Texas Chain Saw Massacre* display a level of depravity and domestic squalor that is only matched by the impoverishment of their lives on every possible level, spiritual or otherwise. Hannibal Lecter may share their relish for killing and dismembering human beings, but he would clearly regard them with the same disdain as we, the audience, do. That both Lecter and Leatherface wear masks made of human skin suggests no correlation between them – the mask worn by Leatherface is of a part with his chaotic psychopathic identity, while Lecter wears his human mask with a specific purpose – escape – though he will have had no more compunction than his debased backwoods counterpart when it came to removing human skin from its previous owner. But while the stomach-churning impact of the scene may drive any more considered interpretive thoughts from the minds of most viewers, in its own blackly comic way, the sequence in the ambulance is of a part with the nebulous concepts of identity that the film deals in – one that may not bear too much analytical consideration, but which nevertheless shows the extent to which the through-line of the film has been constructed. Although he sets an elaborate scene, Lecter escapes simply by pretending to be someone else.

NAILING BILL

After the news of Lecter's escape reaches her, Clarice Starling examines the case with the greatest attention and intuits (while reading the psychiatrist's notes) that the first female victim of Buffalo Bill, Frederica Bimmel, knew her killer before he took her life. Starling makes a journey to the dead girl's home town, and learns that she was a seamstress, possessing in her room (to which Starling gains access) sewing patterns which resemble in their shape the segments of skin that Bill removes from his victims. The uninspiring social background of the seamstress is perhaps an echo of Clarice's own, sounding once again the class sensitivity note so prevalent through the film. Standing in Frederica's room, does Clarice wonder if this might have been her own fate?

What follows is yet another Grand Guignol revelation in a film that has more than its share – the murderer is, Starling realises, creating a grotesque 'woman suit', utilising real skin for himself to wear (as per the assumptions-of-identity theme of the film). She makes a call to Crawford, but the latter is already en route with heavily-armed colleagues to make an arrest, having tracked down the address of the suspect, James Gumb.

DOUBLE CLIMAX

What follows is suspense film-making of an order that would have had Alfred Hitchcock (whose shadow is to be discerned throughout this film) smiling in admiration, let alone that director's disciples such as Brian De Palma (and it is interesting to speculate what that director, when on form, might have made of Harris's novel). It is also worth remarking just how adroitly Jonathan Demme has trod the tightrope of necessary excess in his presentation of the narrative. It is a frequent besetting sin of contemporary horror films that the sheer amount of gruesome incident, while initially unsettling the audience, finally produces something between derision and a not-too-serious enjoyment on a pantomime level of the blood-drenched grotesqueries on display. Sometimes, the

Finally, 'Bill'

cannier directors can play on precisely this progression and utilise it to their own advantage (as with the aforementioned Tobe Hooper in *The Texas Chain Saw Massacre*, moving from a minatory destabilising accumulation of menace to, finally, full-on black comedy). Demme and his screenwriter Tally allow the viewer to enjoy the macabre asides of Hannibal Lecter, but when the business of increasing our pulse-rates becomes exigent, there is absolutely no question of laughing at the horrors we are obliged to experience, as in this final sequence.

The notions of duality – principally in terms of double personality – are here integrated into the parallel narrative developments as Demme carefully orchestrates his dual climax. Both Clarice and Crawford (and his associates) are seen approaching houses. Crawford's is very specifically a military-style operation, fully armed, with a cadre of highly trained professionals whose assignment is to capture an extremely dangerous serial killer. Clarice, however, is simply tracking down a lead – unaware that she has actually found the man she is looking for, in a house in which the terrified senator's daughter is imprisoned in a (somewhat unlikely) pit in the basement (again, the trappings of the horror film are presented unapologetically). The twist, of course, is that Crawford and his bulletproof-jacketed men are at the wrong house. And as Clarice's boss realises that they have closed in upon an empty house, it is his tyro employee who is now in the most extreme danger having, without realising it, tracked Buffalo Bill to his lair.

Clarice has approached the house of a 'Jack Gordon', and her initial interview with the man we know to be Jame Gumb is a superlatively handled sequence in which the audience is on tenterhooks, knowing something that she does not know – that the young woman she was trying to save is in the house she has entered – and that her own life is also in mortal danger from the individual she is speaking to. We see her assessing (behind the carapace of her customary politeness) the awkward, maladroit Gumb, and we note that she is unhappy with the remark of the socially awkward man she is addressing (although, as throughout the film, there is not the slightest outward indication given on the actress's part of something we read in her eyes); when Gumb asks of Frederica Bimmel, 'Was she great big fat person?', Starling's measured reply is: 'She was a big girl, sir.' As Clarice suddenly realises that she has tracked down Buffalo Bill himself, she reaches nervously for her gun, but Gumb escapes from her, with a camp Mick Jagger-like shimmy of his hips (reminding us of the nebulous sexuality of the character). The killer disappears into his basement, and what follows is a genuinely terrifying game of cat and mouse, in which (after he plunges the house into darkness), Gumb utilises the night vision glasses we know that he possesses; he can see Clarice, but she can't see him. As a shaking Clarice tracks her quarry around a house which is his home territory, Demme even risks undercutting the ever-mounting tension by the reaction of the hysterical, imprisoned Catherine – 'Don't leave me here, you fuckin' bitch! This guy's fuckin' crazy!' – which has the effect of putting us even more on the side of the beleaguered heroine, as if that were necessary. And as Gumb finally prepares to kill her, the clicking of his gun's mechanism alerts Starling, and she is finally able to shoot him – an action as cathartic for her as it is for the audience, much in the same way that Will Graham's killing of Dollarhyde in the earlier film was.

Principally, this final-act setting has to function on a hyperreal, nightmare level as the lower depths realm into which the vulnerable heroine must ultimately descend. As such, her passing through a doorway into realms of horror must instil a sense of dread in the viewer, and it is interesting to note that this sequence had the same destabilising effect on viewers in early cinema showings as the room into which the two priests passed in William Friedkin's film of William Peter Blatty's *The Exorcist* (1973) – a place of horror which (by all accounts) produced sickness and nausea in certain viewers. The tyro Starling's confrontation with her monstrous cross-dressing opponent is not persuasive on any 'realistic' level, but then neither perhaps, is the original premise in which such an inexperienced policewoman is sent, barely-equipped, into an edgy confrontation with a massively dangerous criminal. However, it remains unarguable that here, as throughout the film, all of the tools of film-making – production design, performance, sound design and cinematography – are fused into a highly efficient mechanism that is essentially designed to say 'boo' to the audience. Even the functional orchestral score by Howard Shore is perfectly at the service of the material, though it is essentially anonymous (as so much of this composer's serviceable music is. Despite the echoes of Bernard Hermann – whom he clearly admires – Shore makes no attempt here or elsewhere, to forge an individual identity for his score along the lines of his great Golden Age predecessor).

The whole sequence is so finely tuned, that had the film ended here, audiences would undoubtedly have felt that they had got their money's worth. But Demme and his screenwriter reserve a coda which brings the film to the most apposite ending possible.

THE FINAL EXCHANGE

At the FBI Academy, a graduation party is in progress. Clarice Starling is called to the phone. It is a now-free Hannibal Lecter, dressed in light-coloured clothes, wearing an unlikely wig and apparently in the Bahamas. He asks her: 'Well, Clarice? Have the lambs stopped screaming?' She acknowledges his question by simply intoning his name. He tells her not to attempt a trace as he will not be on the phone long enough. She asks where he is. It is at this point that he makes a statement about an issue which has been playing on the first time viewer's mind: 'I have no plans to call on you, Clarice. The world's more interesting with you in it. So you take care to extend me the same courtesy.' She replies (unsurprisingly) that she can't make that promise, and it is left to Anthony Hopkins – in his most mischievous manner – to deliver the film's final one-liner: 'I do wish we could chat longer, but I'm having an old friend for dinner.' He then replaces the phone on the receiver and casually follows the unpleasant Dr Frederic Chilton through the rural streets of a Bahamas village, as the camera pulls back to a bird's eye view, held for an audaciously long period of time. Although this final act of cannibalistic violence will take place off-screen, it is the perfect way to write *finis* (at least temporarily) to the

'Bill' meets his match and the lambs are finally silenced

murderous screen career of Dr Hannibal Lecter. And although Jonathan Demme was not to remain with the franchise, he had set a high bar for any subsequent outings for the psychopathic psychiatrist.

MAKING HORROR RESPECTABLE

Establishment recognition: serial killing goes mainstream on Oscar night

If – as is unarguably the case – Jonathan Demme's film brought about a seismic change in the horror film genre of the 1990s, it performed a similar function for the crime narrative (specifically the tense pursuit and capture of a serial killer); rather, as has been mentioned earlier, in the fashion that Thomas Harris's original novel had done for the literary form of crime and horror. The acclaim that the film enjoyed (both critically and commercially) was unprecedented, far outstripping the ticket sales for Michael Mann's earlier shot at filming the work of Harris. Particularly noteworthy – and surprising – was the recognition from the staid, conservative members of AMPASS, the industry body whose membership is responsible for bestowing the Academy Awards.

Film producers and directors have long been ruefully aware that the films which are most Academy-friendly have traditionally been those which have a worthy or uplifting quality (recently, the pleasurable if unchallenging *The King's Speech* [2010] was an unsurprising recipient of several awards, conforming to these long-established, unthreatening precedents). With 'heritage' films (or those in which noble individuals attempt to ameliorate the the lot of the underprivileged or the endangered) as the awards yardstick, the kind of film which was unlikely to receive an Academy nod was the customarily distrusted horror film – a genre which may have long pleased paying audiences but which traditionally earned the stern, pursed-lip disapproval of the establishment.

Inevitably, a crucial part of the appeal of the horror genre is that it should retain a powerful subversive edge, something that makes it difficult for the more 'respectable' media establishment to take it to its heart. The literary world had, of course, long embraced such practitioners of the form as Edgar Allan Poe, but there was admittedly little question concerning the credentials of this much-respected writer (not least the cachet of Poe being translated into French by Stéphane Mallarmé and then rendered into operatic form by Claude Debussy). Similarly, the excursions into the horror genre by such writers as Thomas Hardy and Charles Dickens were considered to be perfectly acceptable forays into unrespectable territory, given the impeccable credentials of the writers involved. The cinema, however, has long enjoyed its huckster image, which hardly helps finesse its more mainstream credentials (the British directors James Whale and Terence Fisher, both of whom brought great skill to their respective screen incarnations of Mary Shelley's Frankenstein, are now recognised as considerable talents, but were summarily dismissed by the critical establishment as catchpenny entertainers in their day).

Why, then, did The Silence of the Lambs enjoy Oscar acclaim? And comprehensive, board-sweeping acclaim at that? Best Actor and Actress statuettes were bagged by Anthony Hopkins and Jodie Foster, while Demme was named Best Director. The film itself won the award for Best Picture of 1991, with Ted Tally winning Best Screenplay (Adapted). It would be easy to say that these wins were exclusively due to the exemplary film-making on display in the film, but not quite accurate – such an impressive use of the medium as was evident would not alone have seduced the conservative Academy members, given the disreputable nature of the horror medium. One factor dictating this sea change in terms of Oscar recognition was the contribution of the actor Anthony Hopkins. It should be remembered that the image we have today of this performer – a man of tremendous range and impeccable classical theatre credentials who also has the charisma and star power necessary to 'open' a film – is not one audiences had of Hopkins when the film first appeared. He was already celebrated in the UK for his performances in classical theatre and in such modern plays as Howard Brenton's Pravda, which those lucky enough to catch him in (including this writer) remember as a performance of great authority. But his filmic experience was relatively modest – a striking cameo, very young, in Anthony Harvey's The Lion in Winter (1968) and the humane doctor Frederick Treves who cared for the eponymous *Elephant Man* in David Lynch's film (1980) were highlights. *The Silence of the Lambs* was to change all that and launch the actor into a high-powered (and well-paid) international career. The members of the Academy were able to spot just how scene-stealing Hopkins' relatively short amount of screen time in Demme's film was, and they were well aware of the actor's credentials; the kudos acquired by any American film which employs an unarguably prestigious British actor with classical training should not be gainsaid.

CHANNELING DRACULA

The film's success on Oscar night may have been unprecedented in light of its non-respectable precedents, but may (in retrospect) be understood as the perfect ensemble of talents producing a supremely well-engineered piece of narrative, with all the constituent elements organically integrated. At the time, Hopkins was a touch prickly about the perception of Lecter as a 'supporting character'. And correctly so; in *Manhunter* there is an argument for saying that that is precisely what Lecter is – the centrality of the pursuit of the monstrous Frances Dollarhyde is the *primum mobile* of the scenario. But Jonathan Demme was well aware that however disturbing Jame Gumb, his own film's serial killer on the loose, was, it was the serial killer behind bars that audiences would be more interested in, particularly in Hopkins's mesmeric performance, which owed a little, according to the actor, to Bela Lugosi's 1930s performance as Dracula – and it is certainly true that Hopkins has more echoes of the lugubrious, weighty Hungarian sate (a classical actor in his native Hungary) than the more soignée and elegant assumption of the role by Christopher Lee, an actor – one might have thought – closer in spirit to Hopkins than the scenery-chewing, unsubtle Lugosi. Hopkins, however, was to subsequently suggest a further, pejorative debt to Lugosi in several eye-rolling turns in a variety of films (from which Jonathan Demme's rigorous control was sadly lacking).

IMPERATIVES OF THE MACABRE

At this point it might be profitable to note other acknowledgements of the exigencies of the cinema of the macabre which are taken on board by Jonathan Demme. When Clarice Starling begins her journey in search of the cryptic clues afforded her by Hannibal Lecter, she performs (as discussed earlier) a truly disturbing traversal of a sinister-looking garage which has been locked for many years, and, we are to learn, the contents of which have been arranged by Lecter. Starling's visit to the darkened garage is one of the set pieces of the original Thomas Harris novel, and Jonathan Demme does it full justice in his film with a careful use of both *mise-en-scène* and production design (even if the American flag thrown over a long-disused car was apparently a happy accident on the day of shooting). The chilling contents of the car are emblematic in establishing – if audiences were in any doubt – the horror film credentials of what we are watching. Inadequately preserved in a glass jar is a gruesome trophy: a severed human head which glares at the audience as unpleasantly as it does at the shocked Clarice. Rather like a similar early moment in *The Texas Chain Saw Massacre*, in which a deranged hitchhiker slices open his own arm, we now begin to realise fully what *terra incognita* we are in – and wonder just how far down this dark path the director is planning to take us.

There are, for those who know their genre movies, some subtle nods in the direction of veteran horror film talents. The FBI Deputy Director is played by the legendary Roger Corman, a seat-of-the-pants producer-director responsible for many of the best (and some of the worst) horror and science-fiction films of the 1950-60s boom in the field. Corman (whose principal artistic success was in his stylish Poe adaptations, *The Fall of the House of Usher* [1960], *Pit and the Pendulum* [1961] and *The Masque of the Red Death* [1964]) is a man whose talent and inventiveness were in inverse proportion to the budgets he had to work with, a film-maker who achieved some impressive work on the hoof in his cash-strapped epics. But he is also remembered as a canny progenitor of talent, allowing such future luminaries as Martin Scorsese, Joe Dante and Jack Nicholson to gain experience on his films for a pittance. Such embryonic talents were exploited, perhaps, but thereby gained valuable experience in a particularly useful training ground, in which 'all hands to the pump' were the operative words. Jonathan Demme was one of these fledgling talents nurtured by Corman, directing *Crazy Mama* and *Caged Heat* for him, and repays his old employer by giving him this small but important cameo.

Similarly, the director George A. Romero (who changed the face of the modern horror film with his gritty and intelligent *Night of the Living Dead* [1968]) appears as part of a posse which Hannibal Lecter eludes. The presence of these two men (who made significant contributions to the genre of Demme is working in) is irrelevant in terms of general audiences who had no knowledge of their history, but the gesture is part of the texture that Demme gives to his film and a recognition by the director of its lineage.

SECOND LEVEL MONSTERS

The actor Ted Levine was handed a daunting prospect in playing the murderous Jame Gumb in *Silence of the Lambs*. In *Manhunter*, Tom Noonan was able to establish a chilling veracity for his monster by utilising bifurcated means: firstly, the far greater amount of screen time he was given to develop the character (even to the extent of a painfully embarrassing but utterly compelling semi-relationship with a blind woman who becomes one of the victims), and, secondly, by the fact that the impact the Lecter character in this first screen outing, impressive though he is in Brian Cox's incarnation, is nothing like that of Anthony Hopkins in the Demme film. Nevertheless, Levine's performance as Gumb is adorned with myriad facets in his brief amount of screen time, moulding creatively the complex and disturbing character that Harris and his screen adapter Ted Tally created.

THE GAY BACKLASH

Demme and Levine were therefore surprised by the wholly negative furore that blew up around Gumb's supposed gayness and transvestism – although it is perhaps surprising that *they* were surprised. In interviews, both men have stressed that the daily (and angry) picketing that the film received for its supposedly homophobic representation of this character was not based on a close or nuanced reading of the film (such vocal protests, either from liberal or illiberal perspectives, rarely are); that is to say, the Gumb character should not be considered gay (although, if the truth be told, the film sends out confusing signals in this regard). Nevertheless, the attack on the film might now be read as congruent with contemporary attacks on homosexuality by the Republican religious right in United States – far more dangerous opponents of gay men and women than a demonstrably (if not ostentatiously) liberal film-maker such as Demme. Gumb certainly behaves in an androgynous fashion, or at least a sexually ambiguous one. Looking down into the pit in which he has imprisoned a senator's daughter, he assumes what might be said to be a stereotypically homosexual appearance, stroking his poodle dog ('Precious') and using a camp female voice to taunt his victim. In one of the film's most memorable images, he dances around his squalid basement behaving like a parody of the androgynous rock star (somewhere between Mick Jagger and David Bowie). Appearing to be naked in a robe he fumbles (offscreen) with his genitals then poses with his penis tucked between his legs in a grotesque parody of the female body. It is, in fact, the female body which is Gumb's obsession, and we are to learn that the murderer's agenda is to build himself a 'woman suit', a grotesque flesh covering created from parts of his luckless victims (all overweight young women), which will help him assume the new identity he so passionately seeks. Like Dollarhyde in *Red Dragon/Manhunter*, his real purpose is transformation, abandoning the physical persona with which he is so unhappy and creating something new out of the gruesome syntheses that he is working on. This conforms to the film's examination of notions identity in all its forms – nearly all the principal protagonists convey a fluid, amorphous attitude towards any nexus of identity: Clarice, Gumb, even Lecter (though the latter's fluidity is cosmetic – his personality is immutably fixed by his psychosis).

Gumb is concerned with appearance, not sexuality. His imprisonment of the senator's daughter victim, played by Brooke Smith, involves persuading the young girl to soften her skin with lotion – he is more interested in the creation of a perfect outer body that he will ultimately be able to assume. But his misogyny is perhaps apparent in his description of one of his victims exclusively in insulting terms of her size. Perhaps the gay and lesbian protests over the film were understandable, but even a cursory reading of the text (both the original literary version and Demme and Tally's version of it) shows that characterising it in these terms is a superficial reading based on only a handful of elements rather than the more complex strategies that the film actually employs.

EXCHANGES

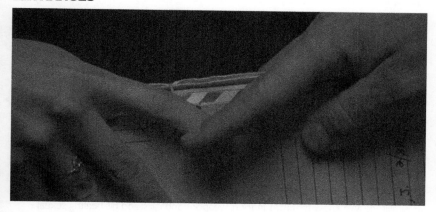

The film's most intimate moment is also its most sinister

What elevates *The Silence of the Lambs* above its cinematic predecessor is the balancing of the two principal (interlocking) plots: the pursuit and capture of the serial killer Buffalo Bill, and the growing uneasy relationship between the monk-like Lecter (ascetic but epicurean) and his novice 'pupil' Starling. The exchanges of this ill-matched duo are not in the territory of classic movie male/female relationships; here an exchange of bodily fluids is not on the cards (although that deeply controversial development is to take place later in the novels if not the subsequent films). Lecter is clearly a man in need of immense, continuing intellectual stimulation and that is denied him by his jailers (the 'stimulation' he is getting is in the nature of a punishment: a spectacularly banal television evangelist he is forced to watch is clearly, for him, torment of the most exquisite kind; it is interesting to speculate if modern audiences in a more deeply religious America of the twenty-first century would appreciate quite how horrendous this torment was meant to be). But the one stimulation for his underused synapses that Lecter can obtain consists of the snippets of information about herself that the psychiatrist is able to winkle out of his reluctant interlocutor Clarice. She is well aware, of course, that such interrogations are all part of a strategy by which Lecter can take effective control over those he shows an interest in, and we see just how lethal that control can be, when the Machiavellian Lecter manipulates Miggs to kill himself (the very infringement of the rules which occasions Lecter's punishment by droning televangelist). All the exchanges between Lecter and Clarice are verbal; the only physical contact between the two is a single moment in which he briefly strokes her finger (Demme treats the audience to an extreme close-up for this electrically charged but deeply sinister moment).

It is perhaps necessary for the maintenance of the mystique (and impenetrable fascination) of Hannibal Lecter that he is perceived as something closer to an elemental force, a nonhuman entity, rather than a living, breathing human being. Comparisons with two other massively popular characters in popular fiction are instructive. Leaving aside the various screen incarnations, Ian Fleming's James Bond – on the page at least – is a minimally characterised creation, described (on one occasion) by his creator as a 'blunt instrument' for the state. There is just sufficient detail to grant the character verisimilitude. We know his tastes in food, weapons and cars, and his healthy sexual appetite is a key feature, but the deeper areas of his character are not explored. This is not to criticise Fleming, as this highly professional writer delivers exactly what is required for the purpose of his narratives and is able to take on board such things as his protagonist's feeling of being emotionally 'burnt out' at times, along with a pronounced sense of ennui, to be banished by the sought-after challenge of a new assignment (in this regard, he is an heir apparent of Conan Doyle's Sherlock Holmes, always impatient for something to engage the attention; and the latter is, as discussed elsewhere, one of several templates drawn upon by Thomas Harris in his creation of Hannibal Lecter). Similarly, Stieg Larsson's sociopathic, tattooed Goth heroine Lisbeth Salander remains essentially unknowable to the reader, although (as with Fleming) there is sufficient filling in of the physical and mental accoutrements of the character to bring her alive on the page. But both Bond and Salander are essentially superheroes, with a totally unrealistic capacity for survival in the face of insuperable odds, along with a resistance to extreme physical pain and injury that renders them closer to Superman than any human being that ever walked the planet. Hannibal Lecter is similarly gifted, with almost supernatural abilities which again and again allow him to escape from lethal and terminal situations. But unlike the protagonists created by Fleming and Larsson, Lecter – while granted a degree of humanity – is (we are constantly reminded) more like a simulacra of a human being. There are, it might be argued, elements of the Jewish daemon the Dybbuk, a creature which takes over the outer shell of a human being for its own malign purposes;

there are shards of humanity in Lecter, but they are in the nature of an outward show, a window-dressing. It is difficult to imagine a more complete picture of fathomless evil ever created in the field of literature, popular or serious.

However in the course of the film of *The Silence of the Lambs* (and subsequent outings for the character), Lecter's various atrocities are always directed towards a particular end. There is (above all else) a simple survival imperative for the psychiatrist: when we initially encounter him, he is like one unstable element of a chemical formula, unable to interact with other elements that would produce a particular change in his nature. This capacity for change is opened up at the end of the film, and when we see Lecter strolling down the street of the village in the Bahamas, we are allowed to speculate on the changes and developments that will now be wrought within him (if any) – and the consequences for those unlucky enough to encounter him (with the exception of Starling, who appears to have won Lecter's respect). In the original novel, Lecter and Clarice meet precisely five times and, on those occasions – because Clarice is sensitive to the nuances of his personality – we see a variety of facets opened to exposure in both characters. Because Lecter is trapped and essentially shut down as a functioning organism (the latter noun is chosen carefully in preference to 'human being'), there is a sense in which the viewer is encouraged to examine him prismatically, as certain facets of his character are revealed to us via the probings of Clarice (her own character, as discussed elsewhere in the study, is in the process of flux and is a litmus paper reacting to the presence of Lecter).

LANGUAGE AND LECTER

The initial meeting between Clarice and Lecter functions on a straightforward dramatic level as a testing arena for both characters as the tyro FBI agent and imprisoned psychiatrist chip away at each other, revealing vulnerabilities (in the case of Starling) and painstakingly prised nuggets of information (in the case of Lecter). And there is another key element to these exchanges: a far more new nuanced and sophisticated approach to language than is customarily encountered in contemporary Hollywood and it is not tendentious to draw analogies with the philosophy of language as expounded by the philosopher Henri Bergson. In *The Creative Mind: An Introduction to Metaphysics* (1946), Bergson posits the notion that language (and directed thought) should be at the service of solving practical difficulties rather than the extrapolation of philosophical concepts. The writer was concerned with notions of paradox and problems, the result of chaos and disorder, and societal solutions might be found in the more analytical use of language, breaking down complexity into utilitarian actions. To a certain degree, this is the very philosophy that the brilliant Lecter attempts to instil into his pupil, but Bergson would hardly approve of the obfuscation which is so much a component of the psychiatrist's method. If Clarice is to solve the problems that so vex her, she must strip away the linguistic filigrees and acrostics that Lecter poses and achieve a clarity and precision of thought – using, in fact, language itself reduced to its essential meaning. Imprecision of speech, in fact, is something that Lecter specifically takes Clarice to task for, even making deductions based on her accent (described as 'cornpone' by an unsympathetic FBI associate); this, in Lecter's eyes, is a further indicator that she is not reaching for the clearest expression of her thought (this approach to the subject is something of an English notion, and, in the UK, usually related to class – a society in which those possessing a marked regional accent have to struggle harder to achieve a perception of 'seriousness' that is regarded as the *sine qua non* of received pronunciation).

Lecter is as precise in his choice of language as a Swiss watch-maker fine-tuning a delicate instrument – and in his education of Clarice, he explicitly demands of her the same precision. All of this is rendered non-academic for a popular audience (how, otherwise, could the film have been the all-encompassing successes it was if such elements were not concealed beneath a fascinating surface?), and the discussion of the meaning of words – which also might be said to echo Lewis Carol in their surreal insights – is effectively concealed by the ever-present minatory atmosphere of the conversations. We know that Clarice is in no physical danger from Lecter when he is in the cell, but we remember that she has been warned against ill-advised personal revelations and allowing the psychiatrist to read her mental processes. But we are also made aware that such an exchange will inevitably be obliged to take place – both for the development of the character of Clarice Starling (which we are keen to see) and for the advancement of her quest to save the imprisoned girl; Jonathan Demme ensures that we are very much concerned with the forward trajectory of the investigation.

A DEVALUED PROFESSION

It is something of a truism to observe that the profession of psychiatry is routinely regarded askance in modern film, and the days seem very distant when psychiatrists were presented as benign figures, pipe-smoking, waist-coated and quietly authoritative, sorting out the problems of a variety of unhappy actors and actresses (usually in an unfeasibly short time). And the profession does not get a good press in the films of Alfred Hitchcock, where psychiatrists are either duplicitous murderers (as in *Spellbound* [1945]) or stolid, unexciting dispensers of exposition (as with Simon Eastland's character in *Psycho*), not to mention the homicidal shrinks in films from *Dressed to Kill* (1980) to *Batman Begins* (2005). Nowadays, however, malign or sinister members of the profession are the cinematic status quo, although close examination of Hannibal Lecter's professional credentials in the film of *The Silence of the Lambs* begs some questions. The assumption is that he was actually a capable psychiatrist, but we see precious little evidence of his skills in the body of the film. Admittedly, of course, he is not practising, but the most conspicuous examples of his knowledge of the way the human mind works is in his sinister and self-serving manipulation of those around him, from the depraved Miggs (persuaded by Lecter to put an end to his own life) and the biddable Starling. A reading of the film, however, is possible which might posit that Lecter (for all his over-weening self-interest) actually has a positive, ameliorative effect on the lives of his impromptu female student, in terms of sharpening and concentrating her faculties both linguistically (as discussed above) and intellectually (in terms of putting together the pieces of the puzzle which will enable her to trace the senator's missing daughter). And although there is no direct reference to the subject in any of their conversations, it is conceivable that Clarice (by osmosis) absorbs some of the psychiatrist's prodigious capacity for survival. At the beginning of the film (in various training sessions), she is shown to be maladroit and vulnerable to the physical danger that her job entails. By the end of their climatic encounter with the fearsome Buffalo Bill, she may be shaking with fear but is nevertheless able to kill her quarry and survive.

Like the best teachers, Lecter provides a host of ancillary information for his pupil, filling in a great deal of background information on the kind of murderous individual that he himself is a prime example of, even though Clarice is impatiently attempting to concentrate him on the one specific case she is involved in. It is debatable whether or not the doctor's insistence on truthfulness has any purpose beyond his demonstration of personal power, but in the final analysis, concepts of truthfulness are of little use to either Lecter or Starling. In the doctor's case, deceit and dissembling of an almost cosmic order are part of his modus operandi, and certainly an integral element of his survival mechanism (in the later *Hannibal*, his masquerade as an expert in Renaissance art represents a lengthy demonstration of this skill). And although such deceit would not initially seem to be part of the honest and caring personality of Starling, she frequently demonstrates her ability at concealing her feelings from Lecter (although he is almost invariably able to read her, whatever mask she presents to him) and she also hides her true feelings from the variety of unattractive men who attempt to impress or dominate her.

In this first outing for Starling, she has to use particular skills that have been par for the course for women throughout the centuries – misdirection, intrigue, charm and (principally) the manipulation for her own ends of male psychology. By the time of *Hannibal*, when Clarice (now played by Julianne Moore) has more authority in her role within the FBI (temporarily at least), she is able to assert it against less capable (and more resentful) male figures. But there is inevitably one male authority figure who will always best her in the final act – her mentor, Dr Hannibal Lecter.

AFTER THE SILENCE

Hannibal on holiday: Lecter as the flamboyantly attired 'Dr Fell'

There is an interesting parallel between the highly successful sequel to *The Silence of the Lambs*, both book and film simply named *Hannibal*, and the recent *Girl with a Dragon Tattoo* phenomenon. While Stieg Larsson's *Millennium* trilogy was being converted into the English translation that ultimately made it such a worldwide phenomenon, the Swedish film and TV company Yellow Bird impatiently awaited the completion of the task in order to begin filming the pre-sold adaptations. Similarly, the legendary Italian film producer Dino de Laurentiis (who had produced *Manhunter*) and his wife Martha were attempting (as much as was possible) to press Thomas Harris (notorious for his measured, Stanley Kubrick-like pace of production) to complete this massively anticipated sequel; the reading public's impatience (much remarked upon at the time as a relatively new phenomenon for a novel sequel) was undoubtedly matched by the film-makers' keenness to create something which replicated the success of the earlier film. When the famously recalcitrant Harris finally delivered the novel and a screenplay was prepared, the most important element in making the film, the actor Anthony Hopkins, expressed his interest in reprising Lecter – but when both co-star Jodie Foster and director Jonathan Demme passed on the project, both believed to be burnt by the gay backlash toward the original, an optimistic spin was quickly put on this potentially disastrous development. De Laurentiis (who had produced films with such stellar talents as Federico Fellini) may have spoken in a comically mangled version of English but was no fool, and canny enough to realise that exemplary though the work of the director and actress had been, it was the public's fascination with Hopkins' Hannibal Lecter which had powered a critically acclaimed film into a phenomenon. New talent was required. Or if not 'new', at least 'established'. A charm offensive was initiated towards the director Ridley Scott, working at the time on what would become his highly successful Roman epic *Gladiator* (2000), a loose remake of Anthony Mann's *The Fall of the Roman Empire* (1964), and a variety of actresses were approached to take up the daunting mantle of Clarice Starling. Hopkins spoke approvingly of Julianne Moore, with whom he had worked satisfyingly on *Surviving Picasso* (1996). After expressing initial reservations, both Scott and Moore said yes to the persuasive de Laurentiis duo, and the machinery was in place for a film which, like the novel itself, would be markedly different from its predecessor while still maintaining the narrative integuments which made the original so successful.

ADJUSTING THE TONE

Both the colour palette and the tone of the new film were different from its predecessor, with a greater emphasis on primary colours (photographed in glossy high definition) and atmospheric chiaroscuro effects – a favourite technique of the director's – and the material's black humour more accentuated, a syndrome which might similarly be noted in the James Bond films that followed the initial success of *Dr No* in 1962. In keeping with the director's expertise in the realm of the epic, *Hannibal* was placed within a much more geographically sprawling canvas, with a great deal of the film shot in a beautifully evoked Florence, the city in which Hannibal Lecter is masquerading as the expert in Renaissance art, 'Dr Fell' (although, in fact, masquerading in name only – Lecter, of course, possesses exactly the level of expertise in the subject that his assumed alter ego requires). Ridley Scott's assumption of the directorial reins proved highly successful, and the film enjoyed immense popularity, breaking several box office records as it wittily opened on Valentine's Day 2001. If the talented Julianne Moore was able to do less with the character of Clarice Starling than her predecessor, this was perhaps due to the extra level of confidence the FBI agent has acquired by this stage of her life; Clarice remains vulnerable, but not as vulnerable as she was the first time around, and professional though the actress's work was throughout, neither she nor her director could produce the kind of touching verisimilitude that was Jodie Foster's stock-in-trade in the first film (another factor here is the enforced separation of the two characters for the first half of the film, and Clarice's minimal engagement with the narrative in this section).

WRITING *HANNIBAL*

An element perhaps guaranteeing a certain level of competence in the film of *Hannibal* was the choice of writers for the screenplay: the proficient Steven Zaillan (who was later to tackle similar material in a succession of adroit screenplays) and the highly regarded playwright David Mamet, a specialist in mordant dialogue. Interestingly, the linguistic trademarks of the playwright are less in evidence than one might expect, and less is made by the writer of Clarice's struggle to overcome her working-class origins (even though in this film, at least one unsympathetic character – the FBI bureaucrat played by Ray Liotta – makes several references to it, some pornographic); neither does the actress allow her speech patterns to suggest the character's blue collar origins in quite the fashion that Foster had. But as de Laurentiis noted in several interviews, the principal transforming dynamic here was down to the fact that Hannibal Lecter was no longer confined to a cell in a psychiatric institution, but his madness and killer instinct had broken free to roam unfettered – although (in one of several clever strokes on the part of Harris), he is not at liberty to indulgence his psychopathic instincts at his leisure, as there are two unpleasant nemeses on his trail: the money-hungry, corrupt police official Pazzi (subtly played by Giancarlo Giannini), who spots that the academic aesthete is actually the disguised mass murderer that the FBI are attempting to track down; and the hideously scarred Mason Verger, a fabulously rich paedophile, who Lecter has drugged and instructed to cut away his own face with a knife while a practicing psychiatrist (a questionable advertisement for Lecter's psychiatric skills – see 'A Devalued Profession' earlier). Verger's agenda is to make Lecter suffer in similar fashion to that in which he, his ex-patient, has suffered, and he has the wherewithal to pursue Lecter.

It is interesting that Ridley Scott and his screenwriters attempt something subtly different from the fashion in which Jonathan Demme and Ted Tally treated the loathsome Dr Chilton in the earlier film in their treatment of the gruesome violence sanctioned by Harris and visited by Lecter on his opponents by rendering them as reprehensible (and thus worthy of extirpation). While the exemplary playing by Gary Oldman (utterly unrecognisable under horrifying latex scar tissue) emphasises the deeply corrupt characteristics of Verger, underlined by his religious hypocrisy, Scott senses that audiences would still perceive Verger as a victim, and thus the character is afforded a certain ambiguity: we do not like him, but when Verger meets his grisly end (at the slavering jaws of the hogs that have been trained to eat Lecter), our response is not simply an enjoyable thrill of horror at a Grand Guignol effect. Similarly, although the fate of the avaricious Italian police inspector Pazzi is writ large early in the narrative (particularly when he disregards Starling's warnings about just how dangerous is the man he is trying to entrap), we cannot enjoy a simple catharsis at the bloody end he is subjected to (propelled from a Florentine balcony after being eviscerated by Lecter, his entrails spilling onto the Palazzo Vecchio), as we share his extreme distress.

The principal difference between this sequel and its predecessor, though (as mentioned earlier), is the fact of Hannibal Lecter on the loose. The murders here are specifically targeted in order to advance his career or preserve his assumed identity (we make the assumption that Lecter has killed the real Dr Fell, the expert whose identity he has assumed) – thus, rather in the fashion of Patricia Highsmith's equally ruthless serial killer Tom Ripley, Lecter is differentiated from the lower-down-the-social-scale murderers such as 'Tooth Fairy' Francis Dollarhyde and 'Buffalo Bill' Jame Gumb. The late Highsmith (with a straight face) defended her killer by saying that he had 'only killed those who got in his way', and there is a sense that this particular justificatory scenario would not be entirely alien to Thomas Harris. Highsmith was distinguished as one of the most uncompromising investigators of dark psychology in her characters, beginning with her 1950 debut novel, *Strangers on a Train* enjoying a distinguished Hitchcock's adaptation a year after publication. In this book, her brilliantly drawn psychopath, Charles Bruno, is a harbinger of subsequent highly intelligent literary killers such as those of Harris. Her series character, the art criminal Tom Ripley, also employs his considerable intellect to carry off a campaign of murders – usually for utilitarian reasons (as he perceives them).

CLARICE STARLING'S FUTURE

Clarice (Julianne Moore) is a virtual bystander to the narrative of Hannibal

So popular have been both the film and novel versions of *Hannibal* that readers and viewers (frequently one and the same) could be forgiven for a certain conflation of the two in their minds. And it is a conflation that, arguably, Thomas Harris would not be unhappy with – if the overriding impression left in people's minds was of his bold, cruel, deeply disturbing original ending. Certain details were perhaps wisely removed from the film (such as Mason Verger's imposing lesbian bodybuilder sister), but by far the most significant change was to that of the ending of the novel. However, despite the radically different final acts, arguably what was achieved was something tonally and stylistically similar in both cases: a grotesque parody of the happy ending. And even though the film has opted for what might be described as a normal life for Clarice after the conclusion of the narrative, so strong are the final images of the character's drugged and hypnotised state at the grotesque dinner at which Lecter (and Clarice's) FBI opponent is served sautéed portions of his own brain that this impactful scene is what most viewers take away from the film. The history of Hollywood is inevitably filled with softened endings when the grim conclusions of novels were considered unacceptable, but there are few which so strongly instilled a false memory in viewers as *Hannibal*. While the film ends with Lecter using a kitchen utensil to cut off his own hand (or, in some interpretations, his thumb) rather than that of Clarice in order to escape the handcuff she has placed on him and escape by 'plane, the novel ends with Lecter and Clarice leaving together for Argentina. She is, it appears, in love with him, a situation created by the use of drugs and an enforced hypnotic state. Lecter has (to a large extent) erased memories of her past life, and she is now a biddable 'love slave'.

Arguably this appallingly bleak ending would have been unlikely to be acceptable to most cinema audiences, but so strong is the film's gruesome dinner table scene (with the actor Ray Liotta's trepanned head and exposed brain) and the memory of the drugged Clarice in a low-cut evening gown in that sequence that the passage of time may be said to have created in many viewers' minds a sort of hybrid between novel and film in which (it could be argued) the novelist's original intentions were essentially met.

Does the final glimpse we are afforded of the future for Clarice Starling represent something of a betrayal of the character – and of the audience's expectations for her? We have been party to her vulnerability and lack of self-assurance, vicariously enjoying her growing self-reliance and individual authority. All of this is cruelly thrown away in the last vision we have of her in the book, and it is difficult not to feel a powerful sense of frustration. In her drugged, semi-comatose state, she is spirited away by Lecter to become her mentor's companion (and, we suppose, lover); quite the worst possible fate for a woman who has striven so hard for self-individuation. We have learned (throughout the films and books) that she was obliged to deal with the painful death of her father, and we have seen her struggling with a variety of inadequate, manipulative males in the organisation she has chosen to work for, the FBI; and her frustration is exacerbated for us by the fact that we are well aware that she is potentially more talented, intuitive and capable than most of those who place obstacles in her way. We have seen her survive confrontations with unspeakable evil, but this final, coerced accommodation with a monster – the worst of them all – is almost a perfect antithesis both of the closure that Clarice appeared to be working towards and any Aristotelian sense of catharsis (all of the Lecter narratives are full of classical echoes; not just those specifically evoked by the well-read psychiatrist). The very fact that Lecter is so keen for Clarice to stay alive is hardly as comforting as we might expect – he has created in her a mirror for himself in which he can luxuriate, enjoying by proxy through her the myriad triumphs over his host of discourteous opponents. It should be said that Lecter, despite his professional calling as a psychiatrist, represents a massive repudiation of any Hippocratic-style oath, and that those who he chooses to take into his confidence (such as Will Graham in *Red Dragon/Manhunter*) invariably end up psychologically damaged – but at least Will Graham is allowed a certain accommodation at the end of his narrative, a courtesy not extended to the luckless Clarice. There is perhaps a suggestion that Thomas Harris had grown impatient with Clarice but remained in thrall to his super-intelligent villain, granting him a bauble at the end of the narrative. As it is, of course, we can see that this is a pyrrhic victory as Lecter is only able to enjoy the attentions of his new paramour by dragging her into unresisting acceptance of his dominance. It is suggested throughout the course of the various books and films that Lecter and Clarice are alike, but this final partnership remains a monstrous thing. The film's ending, with Clarice set free and apparently recovered, is dispatched with so little force that we are inclined to forget her fate (though some may remember the blackly comic final scene with Lecter proffering to a small child sitting beside him on a 'plane a first taste of cannibalism, from his pre-prepared in-flight lunch).

Whatever ending we chose to remember, it would appear that Harris was content to 'let (his) characters go', in the sense that he was no longer master of their fate (it is an extremely common syndrome for authors to claim that their creations have developed lives of their own along with a certain autonomy in which the author no longer has an element of control). But while this final grotesque union may not conform to the more pleasing resolutions of conventional crime narratives, it certainly cannot be argued that it is not audacious in plunging us into the darkest reaches of psychopathology. It is not a comfortable place to be, but then – as Demme's film reminds us (and as did the philosopher Friedrich Nietzsche in *Beyond Good and Evil*) – dealing with monsters carries a very specific danger beyond one's own self-destruction. It might be argued that the Scott film of *Hannibal* is in some sense 'truer' to the characters of *The Silence of the Lambs* (both film and book) than the Harris novel. It might, in that sense, be more accurately considered as a sequel to the film *The Silence of the Lambs* rather than an adaptation of the novel *Hannibal*.

DRAGON REDUX

Once more, with feeling: Lecter gets reacquainted with Will Graham (Edward Norton) in Red Dragon

The arts, both popular and serious, are rich in examples of that 'one venture too far' in which a perfectly achieved body of work is dispiritingly undermined by various attempts to continue milking a particular format. And there are those who feel that there are few examples of the syndrome more egregious than the two most recent films featuring Hannibal Lecter (having said that, there are those who would even extend this criticism to include the film *Hannibal*, which in its day similarly drew criticism for being one trip too many to the well). The producer Dino De Laurentiis had first refusal on the rights to the book as part of his deal in purchasing *Red Dragon*, but he passed on bringing *The Silence of the Lambs* to the screen when *Manhunter* under-performed at the cinema. He would not miss an opportunity to capitalise on the success of *Hannibal*. The second film of the novel *Red Dragon* (directed in 2002 by Brett Ratner) was – in the view of many – riding for a fall. Not only had the Lecter character been given the perfect showcase in *The Silence of the Lambs*, there was, moreover, the extremely well received Michael Mann film of the novel, and there was a chorus of voices suggesting that there was an undoubted catchpenny air to the whole enterprise, despite the fact that several of the key creative personnel were back on board: Ted Tally was writing the screenplay and Anthony Hopkins had been tempted back into the role of the psychiatrist once again. Several highly accomplished actors had also been hired to play key roles: Edward Norton, replaced William Peterson as the damaged FBI agent Will Graham, and the celebrated English Shakespearean actor Ralph Fiennes was the psychopathic Francis Dollarhyde. Set against these plusses, however, was the reputation of the director Brett Ratner, a perfectly efficient fashioner of popular entertainment (such as the 1998 Jackie Chan action comedy *Rush Hour*), but unquestionably not a film-maker to rival the much more highly thought of Jonathan Demme. The auguries here were not auspicious, and many of the critical responses to the film appeared to have been written in advance – for some people, this was a foredoomed enterprise, a second adaptation of the Harris novel which simply should not have been attempted. But, in fact, an examination of the film of *Red Dragon* demonstrates that these judgments did not tell the whole story.

Interestingly, in terms of tone, the film achieved something closer to the original Demme film than that attempted by Ridley Scott in *Hannibal*; that is to say, a more low-key and unsettling timbre as opposed to the more operatic, outrageous *Hannibal* in which the level of gruesomeness was so extreme as to become blackly comic. It might be argued that there is something of a sense of strain in Hopkins performance in Ratner's film; the actor trying to avoid taking an approach which would have been (one suspects) readily accepted by the director – i.e. a more tongue-in-cheek cheek manner than was apparent in the first film, though the dialogue in *Red Dragon* is more straightforwardly macabre/humorous. A new pre-credits sequence (not in *Manhunter*) establishes this cleverly (as well as indicating the extra screen time to be allocated to the doctor): Lecter makes a knife-wielding adjustment to the ranks of the symphony orchestra he is a patron of (to improve the less-than-ideal woodwind section).

Edward Norton, while always an interesting actor, stresses the mentally vulnerable condition of the Will Graham character in a more conspicuous fashion than his predecessor, suggesting that he was channelling Lee Strasberg's Actors' Studio rather than the more subtle delineation of the original Harris FBI agent. But the interaction between the two men, Graham and Lecter, still carries a charge, and Ratner – who, for all his conventional approach, is always professional and efficient – fashions an authentically tense vehicle for the bruising face-offs between the protagonists. The disadvantages that the director laboured under were varied. Inevitably, there was the fact that not only would audiences now be familiar with the Thomas Harris novel (the sales of which by this point in the film franchise were astronomical) but many would also be familiar with *Manhunter*, which had acquired a retrospective must-see reputation for many viewers, post-*Silence*. And by now the notion of restricting Lecter's screen time (à la *Manhunter*) was firmly in the past, and the pre-determined greater exposure of the character inevitably resulted in the law of diminishing returns kicking in. But the sheer professionalism of all involved in *Red Dragon* largely ensured that the perils of over-familiarity were generally kept at bay.

In terms of subtext and psychological underpinnings, Ratner evinces little interest in incorporating such finessing, and what momentum the film possesses lies strictly in its function as a slick piece of popular entertainment. Certainly, the investigative/detective elements of the narrative are dispatched with some panache, and there are of several striking innovations such as the admirably staged pre-credits sequence featuring Lecter and Will Graham that sets the tone perfectly. One particular caveat is similar in nature to the use of the mature performer Judi Dench in the reboot of the James Bond franchise with Daniel Craig. Having played 'M' since the first Pierce Brosnan Bond outing, *GoldenEye* (1995), Dench now appears markedly older despite the fact that Craig's first appearance in the role, *Casino Royale* (2006), is actually an 'origins' story (how Bond got his 007 'license to kill' classification). In *Red Dragon*, Anthony Hopkins – who had already looked decidedly older and less svelte in his second appearance as Hannibal – simply could not carry off the fact that this is a chronologically earlier encounter with a much younger Lecter. But Hopkins' nonpareil acting abilities go hand-in-hand with the knowledge that his skills at seducing an audience are similarly persuasive. Other virtues included a typically scene-stealing cameo by the always reliable Philip Seymour Hoffman as a luckless journalist and Ralph Fiennes as the secondary madman The Tooth Fairy (the actor, despite his matinee idol looks, is always memorable in villainous roles, none more so than in the Harry Potter series). If, finally, the film of *Red Dragon* is a failure, that fact has to be laid at the door of its efficient but workaday director. But its virtues are there to be discerned, and viewed in a generous light, it is not a discreditable entry in the franchise.

HANNIBAL RISING

The knives were out for Thomas Harris with quite as much deadly intent as Hannibal Lecter ever harboured for his victims by the time of *Hannibal Rising*. After all, you can't be the world's bestselling thriller writer (along with the ubiquitous Dan Brown, whose books seem very sedate affairs in comparison) without people wanting you to fail – such is human nature. And *Hannibal Rising* (published in 2006), telling us about Lecter's early years (and how he became the monster we know), was sufficiently different from what we expect from the author for it to draw hostile reactions from some critics, whatever the actual merits of the book might be.

Hannibal, the previous outing for Dr Lecter, had a controversial ending (as discussed above), with Clarice Sterling forced into a drugged sexual relationship with her suave tormentor, and it was initially presumed that the following book had to somehow resolve that unpleasant cliffhanger. But that's precisely what *Hannibal Rising* didn't do. We are taken back to Lecter's boyhood amid the bloodshed of World War II. The young Hannibal watches his family slaughtered by the Nazis. But worse than this, something appalling happens to his beloved little sister at the hands of some truly unpleasant Nazi collaborators. The stage is set for massive, bloody revenge, as Hannibal tracks the men down.

Although the adult Lecter is in embryo here, the strategy of the book (written with an eye to the film which followed swiftly) conforms to a pattern we had now come to expect from Harris. However unspeakable Hannibal's actions (and halfway through the book, there's an act of violence with a sword that will give the squeamish some nasty moments), he's usually up against individuals even worse than (or at least as bad as) he is – such as his self-mutilated nemesis in the previous novel. Does this sleight-of-hand work? Can we enjoy Hannibal's gore-splattered revenge because it's not perpetrated against people like you or me, but against other monsters? That's up to the flexibility of the reader's own particular moral code. What critics of the book pounced upon was its relative straightforwardness, compared with the dense, fragmented novels that preceded it. Everything here is subordinated to a linear tale of revenge, without the elements that made the other books so impressive: the contrasting of his murderous protagonist with vulnerable, conflicted 'normal' opponents. The French copper here is a rudimentarily drawn figure, not given enough space to develop – something very uncharacteristic of this punctilious author. Hannibal's motives and thought processes beyond simple revenge are not described. The articulacy of the adult Lecter is sorely missed. But Harris is much too good a novelist not to ensure that this is a mesmerising read; everything (including the temporal sweep of the novel from wartime horrors to the civilised post-war Paris where Hannibal elects to live) is evoked with masterly skill. Yet the Hannibal story remains unresolved.

HANNIBAL RISING ON FILM

Getting a taste for it: Gaspard Ulliel as the young Lecter in Hannibal Rising

It might have been anticipated that the inevitable film of *Hannibal Rising* would receive decidedly mixed reviews, given the controversial reception accorded to the novel. Apart from anything else, if the film (capably directed by Peter Webber) was to do justice to the book, it would have been expected to reproduce both the merits and the demerits of the original – although a tightening-up process can profitably take place in the transition process from novel to film. (The interminable, and impenetrable, details of a financial scam that advanced the plot not a whit in Stieg Larsson's novel *The Girl with the Dragon Tattoo* were wisely excised for both the Swedish [2010] and American [2011] film versions of the novel.)

In the event (in commercial terms at least), *Hannibal Rising* enjoyed a less enthusiastic audience reception than did the preceding films in the sequence, and at its opening in United States, it did respectable business before dropping out of the top ten US grossing films in the third week of its release. This fifth (and, so far, final) film to feature the cannibalistic doctor describes the evolution and young manhood of Lecter, with *joli laid* French actor Gaspard Ulliel in the title role. The principal interest of the film for admirers of Thomas Harris was inevitably the fact that the writer himself had written the screenplay, but in the event (as criticisms of the novel had suggested that Harris had disappointingly come to regard his creation as a mere moneymaking franchise), this particular aspect had perhaps lost some of its lustre. It is important, however, not to be too precious in this matter. Harris (had the famously close-mouthed author been prepared to discuss his work) would hardly be likely to talk about his literary pretensions; the Hannibal books remain – above all else – perfectly crafted, intelligent popular genre fiction, clearly designed as reader-pleasing mechanisms. If the books were designed to make money, there is nothing wrong with that – particularly given that Harris was able to freight many literary qualities into what are essentially populist, generic works.

BOYHOOD TRAUMAS

Director Peter Webber, previously known for the film of Tracy Chevalier's *The Girl with a Pearl Earring* (2003), proved to be an efficient craftsman, not dissimilar to the film-maker who had tackled the last Hannibal outing, Brett Ratner. The film was made in the Barrandov Studios in Prague (once again for the Dino de Laurentiis company) and is notably effective in the early scenes set in the last days of World War II. The eight-year-old Hannibal (played by Aaran Thomas) is living in a sylvan Lithuanian countryside with his blue-blooded family. When Lecter and his younger sister Mischa escape from the encroaching German troops into the countryside, a nightmare begins which is initiated by a slaughter committed by six Lithuanian militia soldiers. When the militia men invade the palatial estate of Lecter's family, and Lecter and Mischa hide in the family's Lodge, the invaders perform the action which we realise ultimately turns Lecter into the adult monster that we have known in the preceding films – they kill and eat Lecter's beloved sister in front of him (he is himself involved in the cannibalism) before he escapes and is discovered by Soviet soldiers.

As the young adult Lecter embarks on the murderous regime that is to be his default lifestyle, it is certainly apparent (at least in the more straightforward trajectory of the film) that this evolution of a homicidal fiend in terms of strictly psychoanalytic cause-and-effect is somewhat reductive; the ultimate mystery of Lecter, promulgated by the fact that in neither the books nor the films is he a remotely realistic figure, becomes far less intriguing when we are presented with a relatively straightforward narrative of psychological trauma. When Lecter is again living in his family's castle (which has become a Soviet orphanage), now mute after the traumatic effects of the horror he has experienced, he escapes and re-emerges in Paris with his aunt, the enigmatic, elegant Lady Murasaki (played by Gong Li). We are drawn closer to the surrealistic, dreamlike world in which Lecter moves, and some of the energy generated by his endless capacity for bloody slaughter is captured by director Webber and his actors (although Gaspard Ulliel is never really able to render the character more than superficially plausible). And, ultimately, we are in the familiar territory of Lecter performing a variety of gruesome murders motivated by the casual discourtesy of those he encounters, such as a butcher who makes an ill-advised, racially motivated remark about Lady Murasaki (for this discourtesy, Lecter slices the butcher's stomach, arm and back with a ceremonial weapon before decapitating him – Lady Murasaki adds a final flourish by carving a swastika into the forehead of a decapitated head). And once again we have the foredoomed pursuit by a policeman, the French Inspector Popil (played by Dominic West, who achieved fame in the TV crime drama *The Wire*); as we know from the previous books and films, the only opponents who stand a chance against the indefatigable Lecter are Will Graham and Clarice Starling. Copious bloodletting inevitably follows.

To some degree, as with the preceding *Red Dragon*, the film (when viewed in a charitable and generous frame of mind) functions efficiently as a glossy and entertaining catalogue of murderous set pieces – and Harris, always a writer of great skill and instinct in terms of construction, perfectly tailored the novel to the filmic demands of the screenplay (there are significant changes such as the fact that Lecter's uncle is not killed in the war, but returns to the Lithuanian orphanage and is responsible for the boy coming to France; similarly, a subplot involving Inspector Popil in pursuit of stolen paintings is removed as are a variety of secondary characters).

Inevitably, as the book is set further back in time, we are not provided with the necessary resolution after the frustrating ending of the book *Hannibal*, but there are a variety of other compensations here, such as the novelist's always impeccable way with dialogue. But without the charismatic playing of the talents available to earlier directors director Webber is not able to justify the lengthy running time of the film (121 minutes). And if *Hannibal Rising* is to be the last we see of Hannibal Lecter, it is perhaps necessary to invoke TS Eliot and observe that the psychiatrist's bloodstained career ends not with a bang but with a whimper.

LECTER'S PROGENY

It might be argued that far from being a destabilising force in an ordered world (and a force of chaos threatening the status quo), the figure of the hyper-intelligent serial killer is actually – and counter-intuitively – something of a comforting figure. Serial killers in the real world often are often in the mould of Ed Gein or the British mass-murderers Fred West and Peter Sutcliffe, who, while able to (fitfully) maintain a public image that deflected attention from their homicidal activities, are hardly sophisticated aesthetes. Their presence in a world in which we all move is genuinely unsettling. But the character of Hannibal Lecter is comforting precisely because we always appreciate that he is to a great extent the stuff of fantasy. Not only is he the possessor of a towering intellect and a highly developed appreciation of the fine arts, he has a well-honed survival instinct (and set of physical abilities) to match a crack member of an SAS team (despite the fact that in most of his film outings he is played by a not conspicuously fit-looking middle-aged actor). But precisely because this figure so clearly resides in a fictional universe – and acts in carefully prescribed, logical (if surreal) fashion – it is a relatively straightforward task to fit him into the standard scenario of the crime narrative in which a certain set of rules is played out (often with minimal variations) to pleasingly predictable results. While Hannibal Lecter may be free to wreak bloody havoc on his enemies, we're able to feel that these victims are 'other', not ourselves – and even those of us lacking in social graces are permitted to feel that we are not as rude or discourteous as those lined up for evisceration (and, occasionally, consumption) by the knife-wielding psychiatrist. Lecter is, in short, not the kind of serial killer likely to be encountered in the real world.

There is also the sense that he belongs in the category of the larger-than-life super villain created as nemeses by such writers as Ian Fleming; we are invited to admire the style and panache of these fantasy figures and enjoy their excesses in guilt free refashion. There is, however, one principal difference; most of the literary avatars for Hannibal Lecter are customarily destroyed (usually in grotesque and outrageous fashion) by the end of their respective narratives, so that a sense of closure is afforded to the viewer/ reader. Thomas Harris – and, accordingly those who have made the film adaptations of his books – denies us this sense of evil extirpated, possibly a conscious strategy to avoid pigeonholing. It is a strategy to be found elsewhere – the writer/producer David Chase, having created the murderous gangster Tony Soprano in the HBO production *The Sopranos* (2001– 07) afforded the character multiple killings, but declined to provide any appropriate Macbeth-style bloody ending for his gangster, terminating the series with a provocative open ending that asked more questions than it answered. Chase's decision, while applauded for its unorthodox untidiness, was controversial, as has been Thomas Harris's similar strategy (so far) in failing to put an end to his monster. Even more contentiously, the last time we have seen Lecter – in either a novel or a film – he is enjoying the fruits of his psychopathic labours, largely untroubled and untrammelled.

The influence of the film of *The Silence of the Lambs* on the horror (and thriller) genre has been considerable, not just on individual films (as discussed below), but in terms of broadening the parameters audiences have come to expect – both in terms of material that might fundamentally disturb, but also in raising the bar for an intelligent approach to genre material. The sophistication of the Lecter character might be said to be a metaphor for the extra levels of nuance which became the norm for the most accomplished entries in the field – no longer were rudimentary characterisations of the heroes and villains of such films the yardstick, or even a straightforwardly Manichean attitude to notions of good and evil. A more ambitious and richly textured approach became the norm, as discussed below.

Strikingly individual (and appropriately stylish) fare was on hand with Mary Harron's film of Brett Easton Ellis's highly controversial *American Psycho* (2000), a book that had been turned down by some publishers for its extreme (and frequent) violence, the author's reputation notwithstanding. A pre-Batman Christian Bale plays the fashion obsessed mass murderer Patrick Bateman in insouciant, affectless manner in a film fully aware of its dualistic, in-thrall attitude to surface and appearance. But the earlier, equally distinctive (if very different) *Henry: Portrait of a Serial Killer* (John McNaughton, 1986) firmly located its depraved, quietly spoken murderer in blue-collar territory (with some acute incidental commentary of what might now be seen as reality TV programming) and, as with the 2010 Michael Winterbottom film version of Jim Thompson's bleak *The Killer Inside Me*, a certain untutored native intelligence was the key to the central character rather than a intellectual and aesthetic qualities of Hannibal Lecter. But the legacy of

Thomas Harris's character – in screen terms at least – survived in a handful of films that matched impeccable writing and direction with some truly idiosyncratic and offkilter playing, two of them directed by the talented David Fincher.

FINCHER JOINS THE FRAY

'This isn't going to have a happy ending': Detectives Somerset (Morgan Freeman) and Mills (Brad Pitt),
Se7en

The first of these (in the wake of Lecter's all-conquering success) was David Fincher's *Se7en* (1995 – the title a reference to the 'Seven Deadly Sins') in which the quiet serial killer, John Doe, could not have been further from the charismatic model created by Anthony Hopkins. As played (with understated brilliance) by Kevin Spacey, Doe is an insignificant, barely noticeable presence, quite prepared to bloodily remove his own fingerprints in order to evade capture. What he shares with Lecter is a predilection for elaborate, baffling and erudite games not dissimilar in their bookish references to those forged by the psychiatrist. On the trail of this intelligent (if barely visible), malign presence is a detective played by Brad Pitt, and it is to the credit of the actor (as well as his director) that his starry presence is subsumed to create, in the character of Detective Mills, a protagonist who seems to possess pig-headed single-mindedness rather than charisma; any grandstanding on the part of its star would have unbalanced the carefully constructed scenario fashioned by Fincher and screenwriter Kevin Andrew Walker, which, while not precisely echoing the tyro FBI agent/super intelligent criminal antithesis of *The Silence of the Lambs*, still made a determined effort to distance itself from the glossier, more superficial product that Hollywood customarily traded in with its gloomy visuals and nihilistic narrative.

The initial concept of the film was apparently constructed along more quotidian lines, but the involvement of David Fincher was arguably the sand in the oyster that produced the resulting pearl, and in Brad Pitt he found both a powerful ally (Pitt fought to retain the unpalatable logic of the script's climax over the producers' concerns) and an ongoing artistic collaboration that evokes that between Scorsese and De Niro. In the twenty-first century, with a string of ambitious and interesting films to his credit – notably *Fight Club* (1999), *Zodiac* (2007, discussed later) and the 2011 American version of Stieg Larsson's *The Girl with the Dragon Tattoo* – it is necessary to remember a time when Fincher did not enjoy the acclaim that is now his due. In fact the Fincher film that preceded *Se7en* was the second sequel to Ridley Scott's *Alien* (1979), *Alien 3* (1992), a misconceived and benighted project that put this particular franchise firmly in the doldrums for some years. With the new serial killer film, Fincher was aware that he had to produce something very special indeed to redeem his reputation – a task he accomplished with genuine panache. One element that we now regard as a *de rigueur* part of the director's battery of effects is firmly in place: the highly impressive, hard-edged cinematography in which even the most uninspiring cityscape is given a raw and caustic beauty (as photographed by Darius Khondji).

The establishing accoutrements of the scenario are familiar (detective about to retire contrasted with a younger replacement, still full of enthusiasm for the job, finds himself investigating a macabre series of killings), but the elements of the gruesome and the sanguinary are industrial strength here, such as an obese man forced to continue eating until his distended stomach ruptures, and a prostitute hideously killed by a razor sharp dildo (the grotesqueries of Hannibal Lecter's atrocities had found a new lease of life). Of the many elements that distinguish the film, one is its curiously retro-present look, in which the viewer is not sure precisely what era the events we are watching are set in, or even when; similarly, the bleakly existential, dispassionate tone of the piece (with a truly despairing view of human nature) suggested something very different from the kind of conventional thriller that Hollywood directors were most comfortable with. Other indications of the extra levels of texture include the fact that the film begins in almost total darkness (in the obese man's apartment) but ends in broad daylight in the desert, a visual metaphor for the detectives' gradual, growing understanding. And a further *Silence* influence might be noted in the presentation of Morgan Freeman's character, Detective Somerset; erudite, well-spoken and familiar with the classics in the manner of Lecter. Finally, though, perhaps the real legacy of *The Silence of the Lambs* (if it is to be discerned in *Se7en*) is the director's resolute refusal to trade in the clichés of the 'police on the trail of a serial killer' scenario that had seen such dogged service. Fincher, like Demme before him, railed against the notion of the warmed-over and energised his narrative with a fresh directorial approach that was always unorthodox, always innovative.

ASTROLOGICAL CONCERNS

Avery (Robert Downey Jr) and Graysmith (Jake Gyllenhaal), Zodiac

David Fincher was not, however, finished with the serial killer scenario, and produced a further low-key but quietly compelling riff on the theme in *Zodiac*. The director's sixth film utilises the busy newsroom setting familiar from such films as Billy Wilder's *The*

Front Page (1974) and (more pertinently) Alan J Pakula's *All The President's Men* (1976) and fused it with crime drama tropes, such as the pursuit of a ruthless and intelligent murderer. The Fincher film was, in fact, based on two books by the writer Robert Graysmith, who had done extensive research into the real-life 'Zodiac Killer', who plied his bloody trade in the San Francisco area in the 1960s-70s. Graysmith's findings were contentious, but leaving aside the veracity (or otherwise) of his conclusions, the books provided fecund material for Fincher and his associates (notably the screenwriter James Vanderbilt) to create a rigorously constructed scenario. And while *Zodiac* lacks the intensity and unorthodox structure of *Se7en*, there is a close and detailed attention to the texture in both the writing and the direction which presents a narrative-driven (as opposed to character-driven) scenario. Regarding the relatively colourless characterisation, director and writer decided that the dogged investigator/writer played by Jake Gyllenhaal should be a protagonist defined almost entirely through his actions; reactions to his children (whom he co-opts to help him in his investigation) are relatively neutral, as is his mild response to his wife's delivery of divorce papers, which seems barely to give him pause. This notion – the investigator who is unable to see that their private life is moving into choppy waters as they relentlessly pursue a criminal – is an extremely familiar one, perhaps the most successful example of the syndrome in recent years being the similarly personally maladroit policewoman Sarah Lund in the Danish series *The Killing* (2007–2012). But the Gyllenhaal character is not merely a conduit along the path to the apprehension of a murderer: director and screenwriter are able to suggest a certain 'lack' in their investigator's personality which this pursuit fills, while not asking him to explore emotional territory which, for him (it is suggested), is terra incognita.

As in *Se7en*, Fincher is able to suggest an unhealthy, almost symbiotic relationship between two male protagonists on either side of the law. A rogue element in the film is suggested by the more vivid presence of Robert Downey Jnr's counterculture writer Avery, who is something of a destabilising influence. His character reflects the 1960s counterculture (of which, of course, San Francisco, the setting for the film, was the epicentre) and and is reminiscent of the solicitor Melvyn Belli, involved with the controversial Altamont Rolling Stones concert, at which murder and chaos wrote *finis* to the optimistic zeitgeist of the Summer of Love – a pertinent metaphor for Fincher's bleak and pessimistic view of the society in which malign forces threaten the status quo.

In terms of the orchestration of suspense, David Fincher in *Zodiac* seemed less interested in this component of his film than he was in *Se7en* (or for that matter, Jonathan Demme was in *The Silence of the Lambs*), dispensing with all the murders fairly early on, although they escalate in their degree of explicitness. The presence of Brian Cox (the first cinematic Hannibal Lecter/Lektor) as a celebrity lawyer is also perhaps talismanic in the context of the film. In some ways, *Zodiac* might be said to be an anti-*Silence of the Lambs*, which, for all its dispassionate documentary-style accretion of detail nevertheless provides 16 minutes or so of non-realistic phantasmagoria in the scenes involving Hannibal Lecter; no such enjoyable grandstanding for the killer is to be found in *Zodiac*. As befits the dramatisation of real-life events and persons, everything here is presented in a cool but focussed fashion, which, finally, produces subtle and unsettling effects (although there is nothing to match the visceral impact of either *Se7en* or *The Silence of the Lambs*). What the film does share with the Harris adaptation is the sense of the protagonists acquiring an unhealthy relationship with their quarry and his crimes: the characters played by Gyllenhaal, Downey Jnr and, as the main detective on the case, Mark Ruffalo, are all deeply affected by their pursuit of a murderer and demonstrate signs of psychic scarring -- much in the fashion that Clarice Starling (and Will Graham) were to do. What the film fails to provide – deliberately so – is an equivalent for the Hannibal Lecter character.

The principal suspect, Arthur Leigh Allen, is chillingly and effectively played by the talented John Caroll Lynch, but the character is obliged to remain something of a peripheral figure, principally, no doubt because Graysmith and, ultimately, David Fincher and his screenwriter would have been obliged to create their own character based loosely on a real-life individual. One might ask, however, when did such delicacy ever trouble most Hollywood film-makers? (Alternatively, it might be argued that the peripheral nature of this character reflects the fact that Fincher and Lynch's primary interest is on the process of the investigation, and in the impact of it on the lives of the investigators, rather than the actual crimes and perpetrator.)

LEGACY OF THE LAMBS

TV's Hannibal (Mads Mikkelsen) enjoys a spot of lunch

What is the most significant aspect of Thomas Harris's achievement – both on the page and on the screen? Certainly, there is the creation of a massively successful franchise which has proved itself to be both durable and renewable; the latest incarnation of Harris's signature character is a television series, *Hannibal*, with the British actor Hugh Dancy impressively nervous as Will Graham, and the Scandinavian Mads Mikkelsen as Harris's eponymous psychiatrist.

The series undoubtedly has its virtues; Dancy is perhaps the most sociopathic version yet of Graham, with the character's inability to interact directly with those he is addressing carried to almost painful lengths, and – unsurprisingly – Mikkelsen is both charismatic and sinister as Lecter. But it would be fascinating to know just how Harris regards the series – is it anything more to him than a continuing cash cow? This would not be a notion to which he would necessarily be hostile, as the much slighter achievement of the economically written last book (and subsequent film) *Hannibal Rising* suggests – particularly given the writer's participation in the latter.

But with the best will in the world, it's hard to be too enthusiastic about the latest incarnation of the character. In order to mould a typical Harris-style scenario into a TV series and produce the necessary replays of the established story arc, we are given what is essentially another odd couple (Graham and Lecter, crime fighters) in an arena that already has more than its share of mismatched detective duos. What's more, the things that were so fresh and innovative in the earlier Harris books (in which Lecter's participation is both a help and a hindrance to the investigation) have already calcified into cliché within the first few episodes of the series (although Lecter's cannibalistic tendencies are known only to the viewer in this 'prequel'). And, Mikkelsen, though an immensely accomplished actor and a more than serviceable screen villain (as his turn as le Chiffre in the re-energised Bond franchise movie *Casino Royale* [2006] showed), demonstrates with every line spoken in a language which is not his own how superior Hopkins and Cox were in the part, simply because he is unable to find the colour and nuance in the dialogue that his predecessors did, speaking throughout in a flat, uninflected monologue that renders the relatively sophisticated writing flat-footed. But despite all the foregoing, the series is a reminder of just how fecund Harris's imaginative inventions have proved and how even in a compromised series, the narrative pleasures afforded by the familiar plotting still have the power to engage the viewer.

In the final analysis, what is perhaps most enduring about the legacy of *The Silence of the Lambs* and the writer's other books is the permanent (and ineluctable) change that malign screen characters have undergone since the appearance of Dr Lecter in the bowels of that psychiatric institution. Nowadays most ambitious thrillers (on both television and the large screen) imbue their villains with a fierce intelligence and analytical intuitiveness that had slipped considerably as a notion since the inauguration of such characteristics with Conan Doyle's Professor Moriarty. But even more important than this, Thomas Harris demonstrated that popular writing can boast the acumen, elegance and masterly prose of the best literary fiction, and has *inter alia* raised the game of the whole genre of thriller writing. Harris is now the yardstick by which all other modern thriller novelists are judged, and even if he never writes another book, his influence will resonate for some considerable time. Similarly, Jonathan Demme's place in film history is assured thanks to his confident handling of the source material and its influence on horror cinema of the late twentieth century.

APPENDIX: THE PRINCIPAL ACTORS

ANTHONY HOPKINS

Sir Anthony Hopkins was born in Port Talbot in Wales in 1937, and forms part of a line of Welsh acting talent that stretches back to Richard Burton (of whom he was a neighbour) and beyond. Despite the fact that Hopkins' considerable success as a screen actor may owe something to his striking good looks as a younger man, he is (and would claim to be) essentially a protean character actor, which makes his thorough colonisation of one of the screen's most celebrated bogey men par for the course, given his skills in this area. Having worked with Sir Laurence Olivier (Hopkins was a stalwart of the Royal Shakespeare Company), the parallels with Burton extend to the fact that both men were among those seen as heirs apparent to this most celebrated of British actors, with (in their youth) gilded careers stretching ahead. Both Burton and Hopkins are famous for their battles with the bottle, but Hopkins has proved more successful in dealing with his own demons, possibly because he has been far luckier in his choice of screen vehicles and suffered less of Burton's sense of disappointment at his own squandered talent (the latter was all too painfully aware of the many bad films that he had made). Hopkins' Shakespearean roles have included Lear, Coriolanus and Antony, but his first screen role was a memorable supporting one in Anthony Harvey's period drama *The Lion in Winter* in 1968. His first appearance as an above-the-title actor in a standard starring role was in the underwhelming *When Eight Bells Toll* (Etienne Perier, 1971) adapted from one of Alistair Maclean's more forgettable novels, followed by some similarly uninspiring fare, including a spin on the ventriloquist dummy episode from *Dead of Night* (1945), Richard Attenborough's *Magic* (1978), which hardly added lustre to the actor's reputation, though it increased his level of fame. It was also his first serious engagement with a disturbed and dangerous individual – in some ways, *Magic* might be seen as a dry run at what would be his most famous screen assumption. But Hopkins' brilliance as a screen actor was first encouraged by the director David Lynch as the humane Dr Treves who cares for *The Elephant Man* in the sensitive and powerful Mel Brooks-produced film of 1980. Now on a roll, the actor produced a string of beautifully etched performances in such films as The Bounty (Roger Donaldson, 1984, playing Captain Bligh in far more subtle fashion than Charles Laughton had previously done), David Jones's gentle 84 Charing Cross Road (1987), and a carefully modulated performance as the repressed Wilcox in an adaptation of EM Forster's Howards End (James Ivory, 1991). Similarly, his emotionally reined-in Butler in Remains of the Day (1993) for the same director was a career high. But it was, of course, his whimsical, deeply unsettling Hannibal Lecter in Jonathan Demme's film that took his star to stratospheric heights: several uninspiring films were to follow, but there was also a revisiting of Lecter in Red Dragon and a return to Shakespearean roles (and cannibalism) in Julie Taymor's blood-boltered Titus (1999).

One of the actor's most winning characteristics is a very British self-deprecation when his talents are praised; not for him a tearful gushing award acceptance speech (with thanks to everyone from his grandmother to God), but a genuinely modest and winning understatement. The actor's skills have also extended to composition, and a CD of his classical pieces was released in 2012.

JODIE FOSTER

Born Alicia Christian Foster in Los Angeles in 1962, Jodie Foster was one of the (relatively few) child stars who has successfully broken the jinx that so often appears to plague juvenile performers as they grow to adulthood (and their careers, customarily, implode). She is also the first child star whose performance in a film was retrospectively censored in United Kingdom when a new law was passed concerning the depiction of sexual situations involving children in feature films. The film that caused the furore was Martin Scorsese's modern classic Taxi Driver (1976), but before that raw-edged and corrosive piece, she had appeared in such eminently forgettable films as Napoleon and Samantha (Bernard McEveety, 1972) and One Little Indian (from the same a director a year later). Her first encounter with Scorsese was the impressive Alice Doesn't Live Here Any More in 1974, but it was her performance as a child prostitute in Taxi Driver (opposite a memorably disturbed Robert De Niro) that made audiences sit up and pay attention. In the film, the situation involving her under-age character's plying of her trade was already edgy (such as her character's attempt to unzip the fly of the

De Niro character – in the event, rebuffed by him). But the film became even more contentious when (in what Macaulay had once called 'Britain's [ridiculous] periodical fits of morality') a law was passed which meant that *Taxi Driver* was temporarily withdrawn from circulation in order to be subjected to new, more swingeing censorship. One reason that Foster's adolescent prostitute made such an impression was the actress's astonishing performance as the youthful Iris, presented as a rounded character, self-regarding and unsentimental.

Foster's career as a child star was furnished with another hit in Alan Parker's *Bugsy Malone* in 1976, although the notion of children pretending to be adult gangsters has not worn well. Other impressive work followed such as the memorably bleak *The Little Girl Who Lives Down The Lane* for Nicholas Gessner in 1977 and (as adulthood began to kick in) *Carny* in 1980 for Robert Kaylor. By the time of Tony Richardson's fitfully successful *The Hotel New Hampshire* (in 1984, after John Irving), she was clearly an adult actress, but without the understated mastery of her craft which was developed and demonstrated some four years later with a remarkable award-winning performance as a white trash rape victim in Jonathan Kaplan's *The Accused* (1988), a career-defining role. It was a performance which made it clear that she had made a triumphant transition from childhood stardom, and her scenes opposite her character's more sophisticated middle-class attorney played by Kelly McGillis were genuinely affecting as Foster's character began to realise the extent of her own limitations. *The Silence of the Lambs* is now regarded as the apogee of Foster's acting career, but she has subsequently shown her skill as a director with such films as *Little Man Tate* (1991), although she has latterly proved more fitfully successful in this realm. Such later films as Robert Zemeckis's ambitious science-fiction epic *Contact* in 1997, while not without flaws, demonstrate that she remains one of the most interesting and ambitious actresses in the cinema today. Foster has two children, but clearly considers that her own very private sexuality is her own affair.

THOMAS HARRIS BIBLIOGRAPHY

Black Friday (1975)

Red Dragon (1981)

The Silence of the Lambs (1988)

Hannibal (1999)

Hannibal Rising (2006)

FILMOGRAPHY

Black Friday (1977), directed by John Frankenheimer

Manhunter (1986), directed by Michael Mann

The Silence of the Lambs (1991), directed by Jonathan Demme

Hannibal (2001), directed by Ridley Scott

Red Dragon (2002), directed by Brett Ratner

Hannibal Rising (2007), directed by Peter Webber

OTHER FILMS DISCUSSED

Psycho (1960), directed by Alfred Hitchcock

No Way to Treat a Lady (1968), directed by Jack Smight

10 Rillington Place (1971), directed by Richard Fleischer

The Texas Chain Saw Massacre (1974), directed by Tobe Hooper

Henry: Portrait of a Serial Killer (1986), directed by John McNaughton

Se7en (1995), directed by David Fincher

American Psycho (2000), directed by Mary Harron

Zodiac (2007), directed by David Fincher

Printed and bound by CPI Group (UK) Ltd, Croydon, CR0 4YY

13/04/2025

14656601-0003